EVANGELICALISM IN AMERICA

Also by Randall Balmer

Redeemer: The Life of Jimmy Carter

First Freedom: The Fight for Religious Liberty

The Making of Evangelicalism: From Revivalism to Politics and Beyond

God in the White House: How Faith Shaped the Presidency from John F. Kennedy to George W. Bush

Thy Kingdom Come: How the Religious Right Distorts the Faith and Threatens America

Religion in American Life: A Short History [with Jon Butler and Grant Wacker]

Protestantism in America [with Lauren F. Winner]

Encyclopedia of Evangelicalism

Growing Pains: Learning to Love My Father's Faith

Religion in Twentieth Century America

Blessed Assurance: A History of Evangelicalism in America

Grant Us Courage: Travels along the Mainline of American Protestantism

The Presbyterians [with John R. Fitzmier]

Mine Eyes Have Seen the Glory: A Journey into the Evangelical Subculture in America

A Perfect Babel of Confusion: Dutch Religion and English Culture in the Middle Colonies

EVANGELICALISM IN AMERICA

Randall Balmer

BAYLOR UNIVERSITY PRESS

Cover Design by Hannah Feldmeier
Cover image: Shutterstock/Stocksnapper

Library of Congress Cataloging-in-Publication Data
Names: Balmer, Randall Herbert, author.
Title: Evangelicalism in America / Randall Balmer.
Description: Waco: Baylor University Press, 2016.
Identifiers: LCCN 2016006231 (print) | LCCN 2016008560 (ebook) |
ISBN 9781481305976 (hardback) | ISBN 9781481306010 (web pdf) |
ISBN 9781481306003 (mobi) | ISBN 9781481305990 (epub)
Subjects: LCSH: Evangelicalism—United States. | Evangelicalism—
Political Aspect—United States.
Classification: LCC BR1642.U5 B342 2016 (print) | LCC BR1642.U5
(ebook) | DDC 277.3/082—dc23
LC record available at http://lccn.loc.gov/2016006231

For my parents

Nancy R. Froberg
and to the memory of my father
Clarence R. Balmer

Jesus paid it all.

CONTENTS

CONTENTS

PREFACE
Defining American Evangelicalism

Although the term *evangelical* refers generally to the New Testament and, less generally, to Martin Luther's "rediscovery of the gospel" in the sixteenth century, the evolution of evangelicalism in America, where it became the most influential religious and social movement in American history, has produced some rather specialized characteristics that set it apart from the mainstream of American Protestantism. In North America a peculiar species of evangelicalism derived from the confluence of what I call the three *P*s: the vestiges of New England *Puritanism*, Scots-Irish *Presbyterianism*, and Continental *Pietism*.

This confluence of the three *P*s took place during a revival of religion along the Atlantic seaboard in the 1730s and 1740s that historians refer to as the Great Awakening. Although there were localized reports of revival dating to the late seventeenth century along the Connecticut Valley, the Raritan Valley of New Jersey, and along the Delaware River farther south, the visits of George Whitefield, an Anglican itinerant preacher, to the American colonies provided the catalyst. Despite the persistence of some ethnic and theological differences, all manifestations of the Great Awakening emphasized the necessity of some kind of conversion followed by a piety that was warmhearted and experiential—or, in the argot of the day, "experimental"—over against the coldly rationalistic religion characteristic of the upper classes and the ecclesiastical establishment. Although it is perilous to generalize about such a broad and internally diverse movement, evangelicalism in America has largely retained those characteristics—the centrality of conversion (sometimes known as the "born again" experience, taken from John 3), the quest for an affective piety (perhaps best exemplified by John Wesley's Aldersgate experience in 1738, when he found his heart "strangely warmed"), and a suspicion of wealth, worldliness, and ecclesiastical pretension.

Even several centuries later, it is possible to discern the legacy of each of the *P*s. From Puritans contemporary evangelicals inherit the penchant for spiritual introspection; just as Puritans in the seventeenth century were charting their religious pilgrimages, so too evangelicals constantly are taking their spiritual "temperatures" to discern whether they are good or godly. From the Presbyterians evangelicals derive their insistence on doctrinal precision, and from the Pietists they insist that mere intellectual assent is insufficient. Evangelicals prize a warmhearted piety.

More than any other group in the nineteenth century, evangelicals shaped the nation's political and social agenda, just as they had provided important support for the Patriot cause in the eighteenth century. They grew increasingly suspicious of the larger culture in the latter decades of the nineteenth century, and the Scopes trial of 1925 convinced many evangelicals that American society had turned against them and their values. They responded by retreating into their own subculture, a vast and interlocking network of churches, denominations, and educational institutions, which shielded them from the corruptions of the larger world. The return of evangelicalism to public life in the 1970s, after a hiatus of half a century, has served gradually to erode popular perceptions of evangelicals as backward and somehow opposed to technology and innovation. Evangelicals, in fact, have consistently been pioneers in mass communications—the open-air preaching in the eighteenth century, which prefigured the Patriot rhetoric during the Revolution; the Methodist circuits on the frontier, which anticipated grassroots political organizations; and the adroit use of broadcast media in the twentieth century, from the radio preachers of the twenties to the televangelists of the seventies, which provided a model for such acknowledged masters of political communication as Franklin Roosevelt and Ronald Reagan.

Evangelicalism—from the revival tradition of the eighteenth and nineteenth centuries to the militant fundamentalism of the 1920s to pentecostalism with its emphasis on speaking in tongues and other gifts of the Holy Spirit—is deeply imbedded in American life, in part because of its promise of salvation, intimacy with God, and a community of fellow believers. It is a large and internally diverse movement that, according to polling data, makes up anywhere from 25 to 46 percent of the population in the United States.

Although some scholars have devised elaborate, technical definitions of the term *evangelical*, I prefer a simple, three-part (trinitarian!) definition. First, an evangelical is someone who believes in the Bible as God's revelation to humanity. She or he is therefore disposed to read it seriously and even to interpret it literally, although evangelicals (like other believers) typically engage in selective literalism.[1]

Second, because of their literal reading of the Bible, evangelicals believe in the centrality of conversion, which they derive from the third chapter of St. John in the New Testament. There, Nicodemus, a Jewish leader, approaches Jesus by night and asks how he can gain entrance into the kingdom of heaven. Jesus replies that he must be "born again" or, in some translations, "born from above." Conversion, for evangelicals, is generally understood as a "turning away" from sin to embrace salvation, and the "born again" experience is very often (though not always) dramatic and accompanied by considerable emotion. It is also usually a datable experience, and most evangelicals will be able to recount the time and the circumstances of their conversions.

Finally, an evangelical is someone committed to evangelism, bringing others into the faith. The biblical warrant for this is what evangelicals recognize as the Great Commission at the end of the Gospel of Mark, where Jesus instructs his followers, "Go into all the world and preach the good news to all creation." Very often, however, rather than do the evangelism themselves, evangelicals hire professionals to do it for them: missionaries, for example, or pastors of outreach or evangelism on the staffs of large churches. Still, most evangelicals will affirm their responsibility to bring others into the faith.[2]

I sometimes compare evangelicalism to General Motors. Like the giant automaker, evangelicalism is a kind of umbrella, with several subsets. Whereas GM has Chevrolet, Cadillac, Buick, and GMC trucks, evangelicalism has fundamentalism, neoevangelicalism, the holiness movement, and pentecostalism—as well as other strains defined in racial or ethnic terms.

Fundamentalism, which refers to a subset of evangelicalism, derives from a series of pamphlets that appeared between 1910 and 1915 called *The Fundamentals; or, Testimony to the Truth. The Fundamentals* contained conservative statements on doctrinal issues and were meant to counteract the perceived drift toward liberal theology or "modernism" within Protestantism. Those who subscribed to these doctrines became known as *fundamentalists*, and *fundamentalism* came to refer to the entire movement.

Fundamentalism has also been described as a militant antimodernism, but that characterization must be qualified. Fundamentalists are not opposed to modernism in the sense of being suspicious of innovation or technology; indeed, fundamentalists (and evangelicals generally) have often been in the forefront in the uses of technology, especially communications technology. Fundamentalists have an aversion to modernity only when it is invested with a moral valence, when it represents a departure from orthodoxy or "traditional values," however they might be defined.

Finally, fundamentalism is characterized by a militancy, at least as it has developed in the United States; Jerry Falwell, for instance, insisted that he was a *fundamentalist*, not an *evangelical*. This militancy—on matters of doctrine, ecclesiology, dress, personal behavior, or politics—has prompted George M. Marsden, the preeminent historian of fundamentalism, to remark that the difference between an evangelical and a fundamentalist is that a fundamentalist is an evangelical who is mad about something.

A strain of evangelicalism known as *neoevangelicalism* represents a departure from fundamentalism. Around the middle of the twentieth century, various evangelicals grew impatient with the unrelieved militancy of the fundamentalists. These evangelicals, led by Harold J. Ockenga and Billy Graham, forged a new movement, one that differed little from fundamentalism in theology but was somewhat more moderate in tone. Graham himself embodied this transition, and he became its most visible proponent. Though reared as a fundamentalist, Graham rejected the narrow, disputatious tradition of his childhood in favor of a more capacious, irenic evangelicalism, or *neoevangelicalism*.[3]

Another strain of American evangelicalism is the *holiness movement*, which emerged from John Wesley's emphasis on Christian perfection, the doctrine that the believer could attain "perfect love" in this life, after the conversion or "born again" experience. Wesley's notion of perfect love freed the believer from the disposition to sin, although he allowed for failings rooted in "infirmity" and "ignorance."

Fittingly, holiness teachings achieved their best hearing in Methodist circles, but as Methodism expanded, became more respectable, and acquired middle-class trappings in the nineteenth century, holiness doctrines faded into the background. Though rooted in the Methodist Episcopal Church, the holiness movement was interdenominational and sought to revitalize the piety in Methodism and other denominations. Holiness—also called sanctification or second blessing (after the first, conversion)—was promoted in the antebellum period by Sarah Lankford and Phoebe Palmer in their Tuesday

Meetings for the Promotion of Holiness, by Timothy Merritt in his *Guide to Holiness* magazine, and by Charles Finney and Asa Mahan at Oberlin College. After the Civil War, it thrived in independent camp-meeting associations, such as those at Ocean Grove, New Jersey, and Oak Bluffs, Massachusetts.

By the final decade of the nineteenth century, holiness evangelists numbered more than three hundred. The Methodist hierarchy grew uneasy about the holiness influence, however, especially the apparent lack of denominational loyalty of holiness people. As they came under increased pressure, some submitted to the Methodist hierarchy, while others joined emerging holiness denominations, such as the Church of God (Anderson, Indiana), the Church of the Nazarene, the Pentecostal Holiness Church, the Salvation Army, or the Fire-Baptized Holiness Church, among others. These groups generally emphasize the importance of probity and ask their adherents to shun worldliness in all its insipid forms. The holiness movement also survives in regular camp meetings throughout North America.

Pentecostalism coalesced as a movement in the early years of the twentieth century. On the first day of the new century, January 1, 1901, a student at Bethel Bible College in Topeka, Kansas, Agnes Ozman, began speaking in tongues. This experience, also known as *glossolalia*, was explicitly linked to the first Pentecost, recorded in Acts 2, when the early Christians were filled with the Holy Spirit. The movement, with its teachings about the baptism of the Holy Spirit, spread to Texas and then to Los Angeles, where it burst into broader consciousness during the Azusa Street Revival. The pentecostal movement, with its distinctive emphasis on the second blessing or baptism of the Holy Spirit, as evidenced by *glossolalia*, spread quickly after the Azusa Street Revival. Pentecostalism took various denominational forms, including the Pentecostal Holiness Church, the Church of God in Christ, the Church of God (Cleveland, Tennessee), and the Assemblies of God, which was organized in 1914 and is the largest pentecostal denomination in North America.

Pentecostal worship today is characterized by ecstasy and the familiar posture of upraised arms, a gesture of openness to the Holy

Spirit. Pentecostals generally believe in the gifts of the Holy Spirit, including divine healing, in addition to speaking in tongues.

Whereas classical pentecostalism traces its origins to Agnes Ozman's speaking in tongues, the *charismatic movement* brought pentecostal fervor—including divine healing and speaking in tongues—into mainline denominations beginning in the 1960s. The charismatic movement, also known as the charismatic renewal or neopentecostalism, erupted in 1960 among mainline Protestants with the news that Dennis J. Bennett, rector of St. Mark's Episcopal Church, Van Nuys, California, had received the baptism of the Holy Spirit and had spoken in tongues. About a hundred parishioners followed suit, much to the dismay of other parishioners, members of the vestry, and the Episcopal bishop of Los Angeles. Although Bennett left Van Nuys for Seattle, Washington, he remained with the Episcopal Church, taking over a struggling parish, St. Luke's, and transforming it into an outpost of the charismatic movement. Bennett's decision to remain an Episcopalian illustrates the distinction between pentecostals and charismatics, even though both believe in the baptism of the Holy Spirit. Whereas *pentecostal* refers to someone affiliated with one of the pentecostal denominations, such as the Assemblies of God or the Church of God in Christ, a *charismatic* remains identified with a tradition that, on the whole, looks askance at pentecostal enthusiasm, although the two terms have come to be used almost interchangeably in recent years.

Charismatic impulses also made their way into the Roman Catholic Church beginning in February 1967, when a group of faculty from Duquesne University in Pittsburgh attended a spiritual retreat and received the baptism of the Holy Spirit. The Duquesne Weekend, as it came to be known, led to other gatherings of Roman Catholics looking for spiritual renewal, notably in South Bend, Indiana, and Ann Arbor, Michigan, but the movement has spread well beyond those venues and into parishes throughout the country.

The definition and examples of evangelicalism I've just offered are schematic and not at all comprehensive. Evangelicalism in America is vast and internally diverse, drawing on everything from

Restorationism to New Thought. Some of the variations, both theological and stylistic, are inspired by racial and ethnic markers. Southern Baptists, to take another example, typically don't refer to themselves as evangelicals, yet I think it's appropriate to apply the duck test: if it walks like a duck and quacks like a duck, it's probably a duck. Most Southern Baptists, especially following the conservative takeover of the denomination in 1979, would qualify as evangelicals.

The chapters that follow consist of what the British like to call occasional pieces. Although some were written as scholarly articles, most were drafted and delivered as lectures in some venue or another. For that reason, some have more copious endnotes than others. I have made some effort to update some of the references, although careful readers will discern that not all of the most recent scholarship is included here.

Anyone who has followed my writings even from a distance knows that I consider myself a lover's quarrel evangelical. I was reared in what I came later in life to call the evangelical subculture, this vast and interlocking network of congregations, denominations, Bible camps, Bible institutes, colleges, seminaries, publishing houses, and missionary societies that was constructed in earnest during the middle decades of the twentieth century. Evangelicalism has shaped me profoundly; it's part of my DNA.

That said, my scholarly passions over the past several decades have been invested in reminding evangelicals of their heritage as agents for change. If you look carefully at both the New Testament and the actions of nineteenth-century evangelicals, I argue, you might find it a tad difficult to march in the ranks of the Religious Right. My fondest, though increasingly forlorn, hope is that evangelicals will one day reclaim their noble legacy of advocating for those on the margins. In so doing, they will regard the Religious Right as the tragic aberration that it was and consign it to the dustbin of history.

A tall order, I know. But evangelicalism—not to mention the gospel itself—is all about hope.

Norwich, Vermont
Feast Day of St. Andrew, 2015

1

AN ALTOGETHER CONSERVATIVE SPIRIT
The First Amendment, Political Stability,
and Evangelical Vitality

"Religion in America takes no direct part in the government of society," Alexis de Tocqueville observed, "but nevertheless it must be regarded as the foremost of the political institutions of that country; for if it does not impart a taste for freedom, it facilitates the use of free institutions."[1]

De Tocqueville was not the last to puzzle over the relation of church and state, religion and politics, in American society. "Congress shall make no law respecting an establishment of religion, or prohibiting the free exercise thereof," the First Amendment to the U.S. Constitution mandates, and this peculiar formula, unprecedented in Western societies, has attracted a good deal of notice from historians and legal scholars.

In 1844 historian Robert Baird extolled the voluntary principle in the United States as the "great alternative" to all European societies and their long, troubled history of church-state entanglements. "Religious liberty, fettered by no State enactment," Baird wrote, "is as perfect as it can be." Although Philip Schaff, a native of Germany, harbored some old-fashioned notions about the unity of the church and the ability of Christianity to "leaven and sanctify all spheres of human life," he offered grudging admiration for the American configuration of church and state, which he regarded as a "peculiarity in the ecclesiastical condition of North America."[2]

The willingness to give free rein to religious expression, to eschew an establishment, and to countenance the ambiguity arising from that configuration has prompted Sidney E. Mead to characterize the relation of church and state as a "lively experiment." Winthrop Hudson regards voluntarism in America and the equilibrium between church and state as the "great tradition of the American churches."[3]

Although unprecedented, the impetus for religious disestablishment as embodied in the First Amendment, historians have argued, grew out of disparate impulses dating back at least to the Protestant Reformation. Martin Luther had emphasized the priesthood of believers, each individual's responsibility before God, which led almost inevitably (if not immediately) to the concession that everyone might approach God differently from his or her neighbor. The very splintering of Christianity after the Reformation demanded some sort of accommodation to its diversity. Several of the American colonies had done just that—Thomas Jefferson himself cited the examples of New York and Pennsylvania in his *Notes on the State of Virginia*, written in 1781—though the established religions in other colonies, such as the Anglicans in Maryland and Virginia and the Congregationalists in Massachusetts and Connecticut, stubbornly defended their establishment status. Other historians look to such figures and movements as Isaac Backus and the Separate Baptists in Connecticut or William Livingston and the Presbyterian Party in New York as influential opponents of religious establishment. Most often, however, when historians retrace the steps of religious disestablishment in America, their paths lead to Roger Williams and Thomas Jefferson.[4]

Williams, a Puritan minister at Salem, grew increasingly uneasy about the continued identification of New England Puritanism with the Church of England. In 1635 the General Court of Massachusetts brought charges against him for disrupting the social and religious order of New England by proposing that the church at Salem separate completely from the other Massachusetts churches. The General Court banished Williams from the colony, whereupon he fled south in January 1636 and founded Providence, which eventually became the charter colony of Rhode Island.

In 1644, responding to a letter from John Cotton, Williams set out his views regarding the relation of church and state. "When they have opened a gap in the hedge or wall of separation between the garden of the church and the wilderness of the world," Williams wrote, "God hath ever broke down the wall itself, removed the candlestick, and made His garden a wilderness, as at this day." Williams sought to protect religion from the depredations of the state, and he saw strict separation as the way to accomplish this. If God, Williams believed, "will ever please to restore His garden and paradise again, it must of necessity be walled in peculiarly unto Himself from the world; and that all that shall be saved out of the world are to be transplanted out of the wilderness of the world, and added unto His church or garden."[5]

In this memorable metaphor, Williams wanted to segregate the "garden of the church" from the "wilderness of the world" by means of a "hedge or wall of separation." Those images have become so familiar that they may have lost some of their meaning, and to understand the significance of that metaphor we must recall that the Puritans did not share our idyllic, post-Thoreauean romantic notions about wilderness. For the Puritans of the seventeenth century, struggling to carve a godly society out of the howling wilderness of Massachusetts, wilderness was a place of danger. It was a realm of darkness where evil lurked. So when Williams wanted to protect the "garden" of the church from the "wilderness" of the world, he was concerned to preserve the integrity of the church from defilement by too close an association with the state.[6]

Thomas Jefferson appropriated the same "wall of separation" metaphor but toward somewhat different ends. Jefferson, a Deist and a creature of the Enlightenment, believed passionately that religious beliefs were a private affair, that religious coercion violated natural rights, and that compelling someone "to furnish contributions of money for the propagation of opinions which he disbelieves and abhors" constituted a form of tyranny. Religious disestablishment, embodied in the First Amendment, Jefferson believed, provided guarantees against such tyranny. Writing in 1802, Jefferson attested to his "solemn reverence for that act of the whole American people which declared that their legislature should 'make no law respecting an establishment of religion, or prohibiting the free exercise thereof,' thus building a wall of separation between church and State."[7]

Although Jefferson carefully couched his rhetoric so as to appear that he was merely providing for the well-being of organized religion by guarding it against political meddling, it is difficult to escape the impression that he was at least equally concerned that religious factionalism and contentiousness might disrupt the functions of government. Toward the conclusion of his second term as president, Jefferson considered the experiment of religious freedom that he had helped to create in the new republic and pronounced it good precisely because it had proved conducive to political order. "We have solved by fair experiment, the great and interesting question whether freedom is compatible with order in government, and obedience to the laws," he wrote to a group of Virginia Baptists. "And we have experienced the quiet as well as the comfort which results from leaving everyone to profess freely and openly those principles of religion which are the inductions of his own reason, and the serious convictions of his own inquiries."[8]

Both Roger Williams and Thomas Jefferson, then, although separated by more than a century, advocated religious disestablishment, albeit out of somewhat different motives. Williams saw the dangers of state interference in the church, the wilderness encroaching on the garden, while Jefferson recognized the dangers that religious interests and factions posed to the political order that he and others had so carefully fashioned. I should like to suggest, however, that the configuration of church and state embodied in the First Amendment—the guarantee of free exercise and the proscription against religious establishment—has succeeded over the past two-plus centuries beyond even the boldest expectations of either Williams or Jefferson. This wall of separation—which more accurately resembles a line in the dust, continually drawn and redrawn—has satisfied Jefferson's concern that confessional agendas not disrupt political stability, and it has also ensured the religious vitality everywhere in evidence throughout American history.

One undeniable characteristic of the U.S. Constitution is the remarkable resiliency of that document forged in the heat of political debate and compromise more than two hundred years ago. It is, indeed, an extraordinary document, a tribute not only to the ideas of James Harrington, John Locke, Common Sense Realism, and the example of such documents as the Union of Utrecht, but also to the daring and inventiveness of a group of politicians willing to flesh out those ideas into a political system that would knit together thirteen disparate colonies. The writers of the Constitution showed remarkable prescience in anticipating some of the problems that the new society might encounter—so much, in fact, that a succession of Supreme Court nominees beginning in the 1980s have claimed that most contemporary legal disputes could be settled by recourse simply to the "original intent" of the writers—but they also crafted a document of elasticity and adaptability.[9]

The U.S. Constitution and the American form of government has endured for more than two hundred years, and that must surely be its singular achievement. One has only to regard the fragility of other governments—like Germany, France, Spain, or the emerging countries of eastern Europe, which have only recently found stability as republics after decades of uncertain national identities—to appreciate the resiliency of the U.S. government. But what lies at the heart of that stability? Surely the Constitution itself, with its checks and balances, its representative democracy, and its guarantees of free speech and a free press, underlies that durability. The gradual enfranchisement of the disenfranchised—women, minorities, and, more recently, hitherto illegal immigrants—has generally served to thwart insurrection.

The First Amendment, with its guarantee of free exercise and the proscription against religious establishment, also contributes to American political stability, because religious freedom has siphoned off social discontent that might otherwise find expression in the political sphere. In other words, the kind of factionalism that James Madison countenanced in Federalist Number Ten more often than not has flourished in religion rather than politics, with the effect that the energy and discontent that might be directed toward political change more often dissipates in religious bickering. In that respect, the disestablishment of religion has not only fulfilled Jefferson's desire that the state remain free from religious pressure, but it has also ensured that religious factionalism provides a buffer against political radicalism.

The idea that religion upholds the temporal order and protects the prevailing political and cultural institutions is, of course, a common refrain in the modern era, repeated approvingly by Niccolo Machiavelli, Thomas Hobbes, Edmund Burke, and various Erastian Anglicans and not so approvingly by Karl Marx and Friedrich Nietzsche. The notion that religious *pluralism* can sustain the political order, however, is a uniquely American construct. Roger Williams and the founders of Rhode Island in the seventeenth century recognized the salutary effects of religious freedom. A "flourishing civil state may best be maintained," they believed, "with full religious liberty, and that true piety will give the greatest security for sovereignty and true loyalty."[10]

By almost any standard, the civil state has endured, even flourished, in America. Indeed, one of the striking features of American politics, as compared with other Western nations, is the steadfastly centrist nature of its politics. Whereas European nations, most of them based on the parliamentary system, undergo periodic changes—new political parties, ever-shifting coalitions—the two political parties in the United States cling tenaciously to the ideological center and try their hardest in a rather comic quadrennial ritual to distinguish themselves from the other party. The very difficulty of breaking the pattern of the two-party alignment—H. Ross Perot in 1992 and 1996, John B. Anderson in 1980, George Wallace in 1968, Henry A. Wallace in 1948, Theodore Roosevelt in 1912—attests to the persistence of moderate politics. The United States has no Green Party to speak of, no Communist Party outside of Berkeley and Greenwich Village, no Conservative or Social Democratic Party that mounts a serious challenge to the two-party hegemony.[11]

What America has, however, is religion. There is extraordinary diversity in American religious life, encompassing every conceivable tradition, confession, and ethnic group. The First Amendment gives all of them free rein; none of them is established; no one need belong to any of them or support them involuntarily.

And yet Americans do. Despite a recent dip in religiosity, only 9 percent of Americans in 2015 said they didn't believe in God, and another 2 percent claimed they didn't know. The Pew Survey found that over 70 percent of Americans claimed to be Christians, and of these Christians, 36 percent said they attended religious services "once or twice a month/a few times per year"; 17 percent said they attended seldom or never. Such religiosity is unheard of in England and Europe, but, by way of contrast, political participation is much higher there, while Americans are notoriously lackadaisical about exercising their right to vote. In the 2014 elections, for instance, only 36.4 percent of the eligible voters cast ballots, the lowest mark since World War II. The Center for Voting and Democracy says that approximately 60 percent of eligible voters in the United States cast their ballots during presidential election years, a number that drops to 40 percent in midterm elections.[12]

In America, then, religion rather than politics may serve as the argot for popular discourse and the expression of discontent. The lack of religious establishment set up a kind of free market of religion in America, which means that citizen-consumers are free to shop in the unregulated marketplace of religion. This free market also provides for entrepreneurs: anyone at all can gather around him or her a following that is disenchanted in one way or another with the existing religious options. American history is full of such examples: Alexander Campbell, Joseph Smith, Ellen Gould White, Mary Baker Eddy, Noble Drew Ali, J. Gresham Machen, David Koresh, Joel Osteen. These popular religious movements, I believe, divert social discontent away from the political and into the religious sphere. As such, religion in America serves as a conservative political force—that is, its very existence as a safety valve for social discontent tends to protect the state from radical zealots and the paroxysms of revolution.

Indeed, religious sentiments freely subscribed to without the coercion of the state have often served to shore up political values and the claims of the state, and it should be noted that religious groups have a vested interest in upholding the claims of the state because of the tax exemptions granted to religious organizations by all levels of government. The McGuffey *Reader* of the nineteenth century, with its unabashed celebration of Protestant, middle-class, patriotic values, comes to mind. The Catholic Church in America, eager to shed its immigrant image, has gone out of its way to affirm the political order and to prove itself patriotic, in spite of its putative loyalty to a foreign entity. All major religious groups provide clergy who serve as military chaplains. Most Protestants have taught their children and their congregants about the Christian's duty to the state, as outlined in St. Paul's epistle to the Romans. Even the Mormons, after bitter disputes with the U.S. government in the nineteenth century, have become ardent defenders of the political status quo and a formidable conservative force. The civil rights movement, deriving much of its energy and leadership from the black churches, was, in many respects, a *conservative* movement, at least in its means. Evangelicals, because of their populist theology and their genius at communication, have succeeded best in this free marketplace of religion in America, and their reentry into the political arena in the midseventies—due in part to their contrived mythology about America's "Christian" origins—has helped to sustain a conservative swing in American politics.

Both American politicians and foreign observers have acknowledged the extent to which religious sentiment in America upholds the political order. Extolling that connection has become a staple of political discourse. "Of all the dispositions and habits which lead to political prosperity," George Washington declared in his Farewell Address, "Religion and morality are indispensable supports." Dwight Eisenhower asserted that symbiotic relationship bluntly. "Our government makes no sense unless it is founded on a deeply felt religious faith," Eisenhower is often quoted as saying, "and I don't care what it is." De Tocqueville in 1835 expressed with certainty that Americans believed that a "sincere faith in their religion" was "indispensable to the maintenance of republican institutions," and he noted that, "while the law permits the Americans to do what they please, religion prevents them from conceiving, and forbids them to commit, what is rash or unjust."[13]

I do not think there is any kind of mystical connection between religious conviction and the durability of America's political institutions, as de Tocqueville seemed to imply. Rather, just as historians of an earlier age believed that the frontier served as a safety valve for social unrest or that a plenitude of wealth ensured a certain equilibrium, I believe that the cornucopia of religious options—and the liberality with which Americans avail themselves of those options—has contributed to America's political stability by siphoning dissent away from politics into the realm of religion. It strikes me as no accident, for example, that the truly radical political movement of the sixties and early seventies, the student unrest directed against America's involvement in Vietnam, eventually dissipated in a wave of Eastern spirituality. Surely other forces—political, economic, and cultural—contributed as well, but I wonder if the plethora of religions in America, an abundance guaranteed by the First Amendment, did not help to enervate the political dissent of the early seventies.[14]

"Christianity proceeds in an altogether conservative spirit and with the tenderest regard for all existing institutions," Philip Schaff observed in 1855. Thomas Jefferson doubtless would have approved.[15]

9

Religious agendas continue to shape our political debates. The identity of many Americans is tied up with their religious affiliations; many socialize almost exclusively within their religious groups and in any priority of self-disclosure would likely identify themselves as Lutheran or Catholic or Orthodox or Methodist before they would identify themselves as Republican or Democrat.

But this is not a new phenomenon. In 1855 Philip Schaff recounted a conversation with another foreigner, who remarked that "the United States are by far the most religious and Christian country in the world; and that, just because religion is there most free." Schaff himself conceded that the religious verve and energy he found in America could be traced to the voluntary principle, which, he said, "calls forth a mass of individual activity and interest among the laity in ecclesiastical affairs, in the founding of new churches and congregations, colleges and seminaries, in home and foreign missions, and in the promotion of all forms of Christian philanthropy." William Livingston, inveterate opponent of religious establishment in colonial New York, had remarked in 1754 that "nothing can tend so much to maintain our freedom and independency in religion as a division into a variety of sects."[16]

Schaff sought to vindicate his claim about the vitality of religion in America by comparing the patterns of religious affiliation in Berlin and New York City. "In Berlin there are hardly forty churches for a population of four hundred and fifty thousand, of whom, in spite of all the union of church and state, only some thirty thousand attend public worship," Schaff wrote. "In New York, to a population of six hundred thousand, there are over two hundred and fifty well-attended churches, some of them quite costly and splendid, especially in Broadway and Fifth Avenue. In the city of Brooklyn, across the East River, the number of churches is still larger in proportion to the population, and in the country towns and villages, especially in New England, the houses of worship average one to every thousand, or frequently even five hundred, souls." And all of these, Schaff marveled, were supported not by public funds or state-enforced taxation, but by freewill offerings. De Tocqueville had painted a similar contrast twenty years earlier: "There are certain populations in Europe whose unbelief is only equaled by their ignorance and debasement," he wrote, "while in America one of the freest and most enlightened nations in the world fulfills all the outward duties of religion with fervor."[17]

The extraordinarily high level of religious belief and participation in America continues to confound Europeans. By almost any standard, we are a religious people. Not so long ago, more than six Americans out of ten believed that "religion can answer all or most of today's problems," and only 10 percent expressed little or no confidence in organized religion. More recently, 77 percent of Americans said that religion was important in their lives.[18]

This confidence marks another distinctive about American religiosity: its lack of cynicism. Even after the televangelist scandals of the 1980s, there seems to be very little anticlericalism in America today; indeed, ever since the First Great Awakening, when evangelicals struggled bitterly against religious establishments and protested the European identification of the clergy with the aristocracy, American history has been virtually free of anticlericalism. This again derives, no doubt, from the availability of religious options guaranteed by the Constitution. Why put up with a minister or a confession not to your liking when there are so many alternatives for the taking? Religion has remained a force in America precisely because of this ever-changing menu of religious entrées.

But not all American clerics have recognized the value of disestablishment to religion; some had to be converted. After reflection, John Henry Livingston, a Dutch Reformed minister in New York, decided that in a country "where hearing is promoted & a spirit of enquiry prevails I am not apprehensive that the Christian religion can receive any essential injury from the greatest scope that can be given to religious freedom." He added that "forcing mankind into a union of sentiment by any machine of State is altogether preposterous & has done more harm to the cause of the gospel than the sword of persecution has ever effected." In New England, where

Congregationalism enjoyed the benefits of establishment, the "standing order" of Congregationalist ministers bitterly opposed voluntarism, this notion that no one confession would enjoy preferential status, although they came in time to recognize the salutary effects of religious pluralism. Lyman Beecher initially lamented Connecticut's disestablishment of Congregationalism in 1818 as "a time of great depression and suffering," but shortly thereafter, flushed with a general revival of religion, he changed his tune. "We were thrown on God and on ourselves, and this created that moral coercion which makes men work," he remembered in 1820. "Before we had been standing on what our fathers had done, but now we were obliged to develop all our energy."[19]

England, once again, provides a useful contrast to America's persistent religious belief and energy. Recall, for instance, John Lennon's offhanded comment in 1966 that "Christianity will go," that the Beatles were "more popular than Jesus now." In Britain that observation elicited nary a comment, but in America it triggered a wave of record-burnings and anti-Beatles demonstrations across the country, the intensity of which made the young Liverpudlians fear for their lives. Ironically, Lennon, a former chorister at St. Peter's Church, Woolton, was probably correct, at least insofar as his observations applied to Britain. "We are not a very religious people anymore," a woman in London informed me during a recent visit, in a tone more bemused than apologetic, "and so we have tried to devise ways to use some of these old churches creatively." The parish church adjacent to the archbishop of Canterbury's London residence, just across the Thames from Parliament, is now a garden club. Over the past thirty years, nearly 2,000 of England's 16,000 Anglican churches have closed for lack of use. The established Church of England draws only about 800,000 worshipers to it services on an average Sunday—out of a population in excess of 64 million. Perhaps after all the internecine religious battles of the Tudor and Stuart periods, the English have simply wearied of religion, but I suspect that the relative absence of religious options in England has rendered Anglicanism rather bland and homogenized and that the English look elsewhere for their voluntary affiliations—to the plethora of political parties, for example, or to garden clubs.[20]

Religious disestablishment and the guarantee of free exercise in America, on the other hand, has provided the climate for a salubrious religious culture—anything but bland or homogenized. Because various religious groups must compete to survive in a buyer's market, voluntarism has lent an unmistakably populist cast to religion in America. This pandering to popular tastes has tended, I think, to elevate form over content and to diminish the overall quality of religious belief and commitment, but it has also ensured a rich and variegated religious landscape. American religion boasts a diversity and vibrancy unmatched in any Western culture, and we Americans, with our passion for novelty and our notoriously latitudinarian religious beliefs, freely partake of this cornucopia. The endless variety and shifting coalitions accommodate virtually any religious species—Western, Eastern, congregational, episcopal, ethnic— and, of course, there is always the possibility that if you are dissatisfied with the available options, you can start your own religious group. The First Amendment guarantees that right.[21]

If this argument has any merit—if the First Amendment has indeed siphoned social discontent away from the political arena and into the religious sphere—it will force a reconsideration of Charles Beard's interpretation of the U.S. Constitution. But whereas Beard argued that the Constitution was a conservative document in that it safeguarded the economic interests of the landed elite, I am arguing that the Constitution was conservative in a far more subtle way: the First Amendment, by setting up a free market of religion, has not only ensured religious vitality, but it has also helped to thwart political radicalism by redirecting malcontents away from the structured public sphere of American politics and into the pliant private domain of American religion.

Jefferson and Roger Williams make strange bedfellows, and it is easy to speculate on the issues over which they would have disagreed.

Williams—a Puritan, then a Baptist, and then a "seeker"—held strict ideas about the importance of the Bible and the need to separate from evil. Jefferson, on the other hand, excised large portions of the Bible to conform to his own rationalistic, Enlightenment notions. While Williams looked forward to a "never-ending harvest of inconceivable joys" in the afterlife, Jefferson fervently believed that Americans would eventually embrace Unitarianism as their religion of choice.[22]

Despite their radical differences in theology, however, both Williams and Jefferson agreed on the desirability of religious disestablishment, Williams because he sought to maintain a pure church and Jefferson because he sought political stability. From the vantage of more than two hundred years, both men can take satisfaction in the First Amendment, this unprecedented experiment in religious toleration. It has lent political stability by diverting social discontent into the religious sphere, and it has ensured religious vitality by guaranteeing untrammeled expression in the free marketplace of American religion.

It may be too much to ask of Roger Williams and Thomas Jefferson to have anticipated fully the effects of religious disestablishment in America, but if Jefferson had even an inkling of this, historians' claims to genius on his behalf are well founded. Most Americans are well aware of Jefferson's manifold contributions to American life—as architect and inventor, as political theorist, diplomat, and politician—while Williams remains a relatively obscure figure. "Why is our candle yet burning," Williams asked rhetorically near the end of his life, but to serve "God by serving the public in our generation?" In insisting on freedom of religion and liberty of conscience, Williams' service extended well beyond his own generation.[23]

2

TURNING WEST
American Evangelicalism and the Restorationist Tradition

The Last Will and Testament of the Springfield Presbytery changed everything. When Barton Stone and others published this document marking the death of an ecclesiastical organization, they signaled a shift from a European orientation, suffused as it was with tradition and history, toward a kind of determined primitivism that would set the tone for evangelicalism in America ever since. Put another way, prior to the Last Will and Testament, American evangelicalism still looked to the east, across the Atlantic, toward Europe and Great Britain, for its cultural identity and its theological definition. After 1804, however, evangelicals shifted their gaze geographically away from the Atlantic and toward the Alleghenies. They looked for theological guidance not from the centuries immediately preceding their migration to America, but, leapfrogging history, they sought theological legitimation directly from the first century and the example of New Testament Christianity.

In many ways, of course, the primitivist impulse in Christianity goes back at least as far as the Protestant Reformation. Martin Luther, an Augustinian friar steeped in both the theodicies of Augustine and the Humanism of Erasmus, repaired to the New Testament in an effort to salve his uneasy conscience and to circumvent the centuries of theological accretions rampant within medieval Catholicism. His "rediscovery of the gospel," inspired by the study of Paul's letters to the Romans and to the Galatians, allowed him to rescue Christianity from what Luther characterized as works-righteousness, a kind of theological recidivism that had set in after Augustine. Luther's reformulation of the faith was not entirely primitivist, for he relied on both Augustine and Erasmus, but he was able to claim that his primary allegiance lay with the New Testament.

Sociological inevitabilities being what they are, Luther's followers developed their own traditions and institutions within a century of the posting of his *Ninety-Five Theses* on the cathedral door at Wittenberg—everything from the leveling impulses of the Anabaptists and the Brownists to the doctrinal precisionism of the Reformed tradition to the calculated via media of the Church of England. By the time the *Arbella* weighed anchor in 1630 and tacked toward the west with its cargo of Puritans, English and European traditions had defined every group of Protestants who settled on the Atlantic seaboard.

The Puritans, for instance, still viewed themselves as part of the Church of England, albeit a people set apart from ordinary Anglicans, who had been led astray by a duplicitous Catholic monarch and the treacherous archbishop of Canterbury. John Winthrop's famous sermon aboard the *Arbella*, which spelled out the reasons for migration, announced that this band of Puritans, a remnant of the faithful, would construct a "city upon a hill" out of the howling wilderness of Massachusetts, a beacon to the rest of the world, England especially. To add to the pressure, Winthrop assured his auditors that the eyes of the world would be watching as the Puritans demonstrated to their confreres across the Atlantic how God intended that church and state be configured.

Winthrop and most of the first generation of Puritans were fixated with this eastward orientation across the Atlantic, but dissenters lurked even in this homogeneous community. Roger Williams, for instance, took issue with the Puritans' self-identification as Anglicans; he was banished for his heresy and founded the religiously tolerant colony of Rhode Island. But the "city upon a hill" mission imploded in 1640 when Puritans back in England took matters into their own hands by capturing the king and the archbishop of Canterbury. As news of the English Revolution filtered across the Atlantic, it became painfully clear that Puritans in England were not paying attention to the beacon so painstakingly constructed in Massachusetts, and the Puritan experiment descended into a maelstrom of reverse migration, recrimination, and spiritual declension.

By 1700 Puritanism was in disarray, but the transatlantic orientation persisted even through the dark night of declension. When the time came for renewal in a series of revivals historians refer to as the Great Awakening in the 1730s and 1740s, an Anglican priest was the major catalyst, and the preeminent theologian of the Great Awakening, Jonathan Edwards, himself influenced by European and British ideas, was careful to keep his correspondents in England and Scotland apprised of the progress of the revival. Even the infamous Anglican apostasy at Yale in the 1720s, when Timothy Cutler and several students started reading a cache of theological works by Anglican theologians, represented a turn back across the Atlantic to England.

Farther south, in the Middle Colonies, the revival there also had its roots in Europe. Since the founding of New Netherland in 1628, the ministers (or dominies) of the Dutch Reformed Church had an ambivalent relationship with their ecclesiastical superiors back in the Netherlands, but the arrival of a Dutch minister in 1720 reinfused the church with European influence—an influence that was not entirely welcome. Theodorus Jacobus Frelinghuysen had been immersed in a renewal movement called Pietism in the Old World, one that prized spiritual ardor above mere intellectual assent, and when he arrived in the New World, he meant to put his Pietistic convictions into practice. Frelinghuysen's machinations divided his congregations in New Jersey and triggered the Great Awakening in the Middle Colonies. Through his friendship with Gilbert Tennent, Frelinghuysen's Pietism spread beyond Dutch circles to the Presbyterians.

European sources made their presence felt in other colonial religious communities as well. German immigrants were also influenced by a Pietism defined by the enemies of scholasticism back in Europe. The short-lived Swedish settlements along the Delaware River sought to orient their religious life toward Uppsala, although political vicissitudes eventually prompted a redirection toward Canterbury by the time of the American Revolution. Among the English, Pietistic renewal took the form of Methodism, a movement that took its own institutional form in 1784: the Methodist Episcopal Church.

Even during the early years of the Second Great Awakening, European influences were apparent. Among students at Yale College, Enlightenment ideas enjoyed such popularity that students referred to one another by the names of the French philosophes (Rousseau, Voltaire et al.). When Timothy Dwight, Jonathan Edwards' son-in-law, took over as president in 1796, he instituted a four-year curriculum of moral improvement to reintroduce students to orthodox Christianity, but the objects of study hailed, once again, from the eastern shores of the Atlantic, not the western. The same pattern obtained during the early years of the Great Revival in the South. As Leigh Eric Schmidt has demonstrated, the Scottish practice of sacramental seasons provided a template for the camp meetings at Gaspar River and Cane Ridge, so once again Old World forms dictated religious expressions in the New World, even so far inland as the Cumberland Valley.

Whatever one can say about the Second Great Awakening, one must say that it was a time of religious ferment and theological reconfiguration. Historians have spilled a great deal of ink portraying the social unrest of the Burned-Over District in upstate New York, an area opened for mass settlement by the construction of the Erie Canal. To the south, the success of the Gaspar River gathering in August 1900 caught the eye of the Presbyterian minister in Cane Ridge. Barton W. Stone organized another camp meeting for the following summer, and the spectacular scenes of the Cane Ridge Revival are forever etched into America's religious consciousness.

But something else happened as well. Within a few years of Cane Ridge, which had been remarkable for its frontier ecumenicity, denominational distinctions once again reared their ugly heads. More to the point, Old Side Presbyterians in the East sought to reinforce European sensibilities—a strict Calvinist theology, an educated clergy, and decorum in worship—that Stone and the Campbells, Thomas and Alexander, considered pointless and inimical to revivals, especially on the frontier, where such niceties counted for little and arguably impeded the spread of the gospel.

In the midst of these intramural squabbles, Stone and others decided to take a stand against these denominational accretions and the European-based fustiness. The Last Will and Testament of the Springfield Presbytery decisively broke with tradition and officially dispensed with denominational divisiveness by positing that the New Testament alone would determine the shape and theology of the new movement. "No creed but the Bible" became the new rallying cry, and all disputed matters would thereafter be adjudged not by tradition but by Scripture alone.

The effect of the Last Will and Testament on American evangelicalism was to reorient it from the East to the West, from a dependence on European forms steeped in tradition and toward the western frontier, which offered a kind of tabula rasa. Following the lead of the Stone-Campbell tradition, American evangelicals have reinvented themselves endlessly, most often claiming inspiration solely from the Scriptures, often explicitly disavowing any connection whatsoever with tradition.

Paradoxically, one of the ideologies that would facilitate this transformation was an interpretive device imported from Great Britain, something called Scottish Common Sense Realism, which would become the regnant Protestant hermeneutic of the nineteenth century. This ideology democratized biblical interpretation by asserting that the proper reading of the Bible was the plainest and most apparent one, and therefore readily accessible to the sincere and discerning reader.

The authors of the Last Will and Testament articulated these Common Sense principles for the Restoration movement. They directed that "the people may have free course to the Bible" and specified that candidates for ministry would "henceforth study the Holy Scriptures with fervent prayer, and obtain license from God to preach the simple Gospel, with the Holy Ghost sent down from heaven, without any mixture of philosophy, vain deceit, traditions of men, or the rudiments of the world." Common Sense Realism placed the Scriptures within reach of the masses, and nineteenth-century Americans responded by interpreting the Bible for themselves absent the filters of history and tradition.

No one in the antebellum period personified this new license better than William Miller. A farmer and a self-styled biblical interpreter from Low Hampton, New York, Miller decided that the reigning eschatology of postmillennialism, the notion that Jesus would return *after* believers had constructed the millennial kingdom, was mistaken. Miller elected to skip over centuries of biblical interpretation and return directly to the Scriptures. Armed with a benumbing barrage of numbers and arcane calculations, Miller announced that the second advent of Christ would take place sometime between March 1843 and March 1844. When the Lord failed to materialize as scheduled, Miller reluctantly agreed to a "tarrying time," which adjusted the date to October 22, 1844—albeit with the same result.

Miller was not the only one to strike out in a new direction. Indeed, the antebellum period was the era of religious innovation. Charles Grandison Finney's "new measures" represented a fresh approach to revivals as well as a brazen repudiation of the starchy Calvinism associated with both the theologians at Princeton Theological Seminary and the European traditions they defended. The "new measures" proved remarkably successful, in part because the notion that individuals controlled their own spiritual destinies comported well with a people who had only recently taken their political destiny into their own hands.

Another antebellum religious innovator was confused by the proliferation of denominations and their competing claims to the truth. Joseph Smith Jr. "retired to the woods" and was instructed by an angel to hold off on joining any particular denomination and await further word from on high. The new revelation, unearthed on the side of Hill Cumorah in western New York, told of the wanderings of the people of God in the New World and minimized their connection with the Old World, another example of the reorientation from east to west. And as Joseph Smith and his followers contemplated the future, they looked not to Jerusalem but to Jackson County, Missouri, where the heavenly city of Zion would eventually materialize.

While Smith and the Mormons adhered to a new history—or at least to a history newly discovered—other religious leaders in the postbellum period, following the lead of Stone and the Campbells, chose to ignore history. Dispensational premillennialism was another import from Great Britain, coming to the New World in the person of John Nelson Darby, but it quickly resonated with American evangelicals, who made it their own. Dispensationalism entailed a return to the Scriptures, especially the prophetic passages of Daniel and the book of Revelation. The notion of premillennialism asserted that Jesus would return at any moment, and in making such an assertion, the dispensationalists willfully repudiated the eschatology of their antebellum forebears. Postmillennialism, with its corollary that believers bore responsibility for ushering in the millennial kingdom, had animated various social reform movements in antebellum America. The dispensationalists, however, chose to ignore that history in favor of a novel interpretation of biblical prophecy, one that disregarded the tradition of social reform so evident in American society only decades earlier.

Another form of primitivism emanated from Princeton Theological Seminary in the nineteenth century. The publication of *The Origin of Species* in 1859 brought Charles Darwin's ideas to America. Taken to their logical conclusion, evolutionary ideas cast doubt on the veracity of the Genesis account of creation and, by extension, the entire Bible. The second blow was the discipline of higher criticism, imported from Germany, which impugned the reliability of the Scriptures. The Princeton theologians—Charles Hodge, A. A. Hodge, and B. B. Warfield, among others—responded to these threats with what might be considered the ultimate expression of primitivism. The Bible was divinely inspired and utterly reliable, they insisted, because it was entirely without error in the *original manuscripts*. Yes, minor errors and inconsistencies might have crept into the extant text through the agency of copyists down through the centuries, but in their original, pristine form, the Scriptures were inerrant.

Restorationism within American nineteenth-century evangelicalism took still another form in the holiness movement, which sought to restore piety and spiritual ardor to nineteenth-century denominations that had, in the judgment of holiness people, grown complacent. The holiness movement functioned as a renewal initiative within Protestant denominations, principally Methodism. Holiness gatherings, centered in the camp meetings at such venues as Oak Bluffs, Massachusetts, and Ocean Grove, New Jersey, fairly reverberated with spiritual fervor. But their ardor alternated with denunciations of the spiritual declension they saw everywhere around them, evidenced by such middle-class emoluments as organs, robed choirs, and educated clergy. The holiness people sought desperately to restore Methodism and other denominations to the spiritual vitality that had marked their formation; they wanted these organizations to return to the piety of their origins. The primitivist efforts of the holiness people were thwarted, however, by denominational hierarchies, especially within Methodism, so reform-minded people like Daniel S. Warner, A. B. Simpson, and Phineas Bresee were forced to start anew with their own denominations.

Perhaps the best example of primitivism in the history of American evangelicalism, outside of the Stone-Campbell movement, is the emergence of pentecostalism. On January 1, 1901, the first day of the new century, a young woman named Agnes Nevada Ozman began speaking in tongues after the manner of the New Testament Christians. The founder and head of Bethel Bible College in Topeka, Kansas, Charles Fox Parham, had been teaching about the day of Pentecost in Acts 2, when the Holy Spirit engulfed the early Christians "as a mighty wind" and they began speaking in tongues. Parham carried news of this phenomenon throughout Kansas, Missouri, and Texas, where it was picked up by an African American hotel waiter, William J. Seymour, affiliated with the Evening Light Saints, who in turn brought it west to Los Angeles. His strange ideas cost him a job with the congregation that wanted to consider him as their pastor, but his preaching from a porch on Bonnie Brae Street triggered the outbreak of *glossolalia*; and when the crowds became so large they spilled into the street, the group found a new location at 312 Azusa Street. Thus began, in April 1906, the famous Azusa Street Revival, which would reshape American evangelicalism throughout the twentieth century.

"In the year 1900, Charles F. Parham, and his wife and family and a number of Bible students," Lillian Thistlewaite wrote in her account of the origins of twentieth-century pentecostalism, "gathered in the Bethel Bible School to study the Word of God, using no text book excepting, the Bible." Parham, Seymour, and other pentecostals saw themselves as having recovered the first-century vision of Christianity, thereby claiming the gifts of the Holy Spirit promised in the New Testament. In particular, the gift of *glossolalia*, which had lain fallow in the centuries between the first and the twentieth, was once again available to the faithful, and anyone who resisted claiming that gift missed out on the "full gospel" of the New Testament.[1]

One of the glorious characteristics of the early days of pentecostalism was its interracial character and the its receptivity to the leadership of women, who approached parity with men. For a brief and liminal moment, pentecostalism approximated the kind of spiritual egalitarianism that St. Paul had talked about in Galatians 3. As the pentecostal movement matured, however, and various factions split off into their own denominations, the early promise of spiritual and earthly equality dissipated, first along racial lines and eventually in the diminished number of women in leadership positions, including the professional ministry.

The fundamentalists of the 1910s and 1920s also adhered to a kind of primitivism. In their battle against the encroachment of liberal or "modernist" ideas, they returned directly to the Scriptures to reaffirm their allegiance to such orthodox doctrines as the virgin birth of Jesus, the authenticity of miracles, and the second coming of Christ. Fundamentalists believed that their theological and ecclesiastical adversaries had erred by allowing their orthodoxy to be swept aside by the intellectual currents of contemporary culture. Salvation lay, the fundamentalists decided, in returning to the simplicity of New Testament theology, absent the centuries of accumulated tradition and distractions.

A final example of evangelical primitivism and ahistoricism is the Religious Right. Arising in the late 1970s in response to attempts to rescind the tax-exempt status of Bob Jones University because of its racial policies, the Religious Right emerged as a potent political force in the 1980s. Jerry Falwell, James Robison, Tim LaHaye, and others, working with Paul Weyrich and Richard Viguerie, assembled a formidable political coalition that, according to pollster Louis Harris, may have provided the margin of victory for Ronald Reagan in the 1980 election and helped to reelect him four years later.

In its quest for political influence, however, the Religious Right defaulted on the noble history of nineteenth-century evangelical social activism, especially in its attitudes toward women. Nineteenth-century evangelicals had set the social and political agenda for much of the century, and it was an agenda that favored the poor and the marginalized in society and sought to improve their fortunes. Abolitionism comes immediately to mind, but the temperance movement, which was in fact (contrary to contemporary perceptions) a progressive cause, also qualifies. Evangelicals sought prison reform and educational opportunities for women, for freed slaves, and for the children of the working classes. They supported women's suffrage and generally looked out for the interests of those on the margins of society.

The late twentieth-century manifestation of evangelical political activism neglected the principles of evangelicalism's nineteenth-century forebears. Despite their labored efforts to portray themselves as the new abolitionists by virtue of their opposition to abortion, leaders of the Religious Right generally have not evinced the same concern for the least among us. By cobbling together a political program that tilts heavily in the direction of white, middle-class, conservative Republicanism, the Religious Right demonstrates a disregard for its own history and tradition. Some associated with the movement, especially during the Reagan era, even sought to justify the acquisitive impulses of the so-called prosperity theology by recourse to the Scriptures, and their attitudes toward women drew more from the cult of domesticity than from the example of nineteenth-century evangelical activists.

What, finally, is the relationship between evangelicals and the Restorationist tradition? The Last Will and Testament decisively reoriented American evangelicalism from east to west, from a dependence on English and European theology and traditions, which had shaped American Protestantism through the Revolutionary period, to a more indigenous, primitivist definition of the faith. More often than not, evangelicals in America have followed the lead of the Restorationists in resorting directly to the Bible in matters of faith and doctrine rather than consulted the precedents of history. Millerism, pentecostalism, and fundamentalism illustrate this tendency. Finally, the ahistoricism implicit in the Stone-Campbell movement has led evangelicals to ignore their own history, be it the dispensationalism of the late nineteenth century, which overturned the postmillennial optimism of the antebellum period, or the reactive, conservative agenda of the Religious Right, which ignored the heritage of nineteenth-century political activism in favor of an ethic that became virtually indistinguishable from the platform of the Republican Party.

What can evangelicals still learn from the Restorationist tradition? In the Last Will and Testament of the Springfield Presbytery, the authors noted that "it is appointed for all delegated bodies once to die." The Restorationist movement properly takes a dim view of institutionalized religion as inimical to true piety. Campbell recognized that denominations are merely human constructions—and therefore flawed; sociologists remind us that institutions seek above all their own self-perpetuation.

At least as far back as the sixteenth century, Protestants have recognized the corruptibility of institutions, yet we repeatedly invest our faith and our energies in their construction and maintenance, despite the demonstrable perils of doing so. Pietism mobilized in conventicles among European Protestants for the purpose of reinvigorating institutions that had fallen into the torpor of scholasticism. Methodism began in a flurry of piety and spiritual ardor, and yet within decades of taking institutional form, holiness people began calling for its return to the faith. Pentecostalism burst onto the scene with a religious fervor that virtually obliterated racial and gender barriers, but when it took institutional form, the barriers reasserted themselves. Fundamentalists reluctantly broke with institutions corrupted by modernism—and then promptly constructed their own denominations. Even the nondenominational megachurches, which initially define themselves as transcending petty denominational intrigues, eventually become denominations themselves—the Willow Creek Association, Vineyard Christian Fellowship, Calvary Chapel—even if they resist the term *denomination*. In another example of misplaced faith in institutions, George Marsden issued an extended jeremiad about the failure of universities to remain true to their religious origins.[2]

Looking at the history of American evangelicalism, one would suppose that the routinization and institutionalization of religious impulses was a sociological inevitability, but the Restorationist movement suggests otherwise. Throughout its history, the Stone-Campbell tradition has maintained a healthy suspicion of denominational forms. Thomas Campbell back in 1804 recognized what Marsden and others fail to comprehend—that institutions, be they ecclesiastical or educational, are remarkably poor guarantors of piety. Institutions inevitably serve themselves and eventually suborn themselves to the pressures of building programs and mortgages, parking lots and pension funds. Nothing is more difficult than eliminating an institution, yet that is what makes the Last Will and Testament all the more remarkable—because it opens with an attestation to the health of the Springfield Presbytery, the very institution that the authors meant to kill.

Stone and his colleagues had the courage in 1804 to pronounce the Springfield Presbytery dead. Ever since, modeling themselves on the relational theology of Jesus and the primitive simplicity of the New Testament church, the Stone-Campbell tradition has generally looked askance at institutional forms, preferring to take seriously the promise of Jesus that wherever two or three are gathered, he is there. Evangelicals, by and large, have yet to appropriate that legacy of the Restorationist movement.

A postscript. I recently had the privilege of spending the day with the redoubtable Fred Shuttlesworth in Birmingham, Alabama. After several hours of reminiscing about the civil rights movement, Martin Luther King Jr., and Shuttlesworth's own brush with death on Christmas Day 1956, when the Ku Klux Klan detonated sixteen sticks of dynamite beneath the Bethel Baptist Church parsonage while he lay in bed, Shuttlesworth volunteered that the New Testament church was the closest that any human endeavor had ever come to fulfilling the ideals of Christianity. He added that the early Christians had been filled with the Spirit, and then they proceeded to change the world. "That's what we were trying to do in the movement," he said, referring to the civil rights struggle. I pressed him on that comment, whereupon this giant of the civil rights movement replied that he often preached from the Acts of the Apostles during the difficult days of the early 1960s, because the Acts of the Apostles provided the best model for Christian action. He recited Acts 5:41 in particular: "And they departed from the presence of the council, rejoicing that they were worthy to suffer shame for his name."[3]

The activists in the civil rights movement did just that. Not only did they invoke the purity of the New Testament church as their model, they did more than disregard history, which for them was a painful legacy of suffering, degradation, and injustice. They looked to the gospel not merely for the sport or the satisfaction of leapfrogging history and asserting a primitivist understanding of the faith. They appropriated the gospel of the New Testament for an even higher purpose: to change the course of history itself.

3

CASTING ASIDE THE BALLAST OF HISTORY AND TRADITION

Protestants and the Bible in the Nineteenth Century

For Protestants at the turn of the nineteenth century, America represented a world of possibilities. The new Constitution had enshrined into law the radical and unprecedented notion of religious disestablishment, which had survived an experimental phase in the pluralistic crucible of the Middle Colonies. For Protestants especially, who were unfettered by creeds or confessions, disestablishment meant that they could try new ideas and theologies and forms of worship without worrying about the interference of bishops or government officials.

American Protestants took full advantage of that opportunity, citing the Bible as their only warrant. Martin Luther had insisted on *sola scriptura*, the Bible alone, as the basis for authority, casting overboard the ballast of history and tradition. That notion, combined with the First Amendment guarantees of religious freedom, gave rise to the Protestant free-for-alls that would characterize nineteenth-century America.

As Americans reveled in disestablishment, embarking on a veritable rampage of theological innovation and liturgical experimentation at the turn of the nineteenth century, the immediate context was a series of evangelical revivals that historians call the Second

Great Awakening. (The Great Awakening, or the First Great Awakening, generally refers to the revival of the 1730s and 1740s along the Atlantic seaboard.) The Second Awakening, which lasted approximately from the 1790s until the 1830s, convulsed three theaters of the new nation: New England, the Cumberland Valley, and western New York. The New England phase of the Awakening, by far the most sedate, was centered in northwestern Connecticut and around Yale College, whose president, Timothy Dwight, was the grandson of Jonathan Edwards, America's preeminent theologian and primary apologist for the First Great Awakening.[1]

The Second Great Awakening in the South, also known as the Great Revival, brought religion to the frontier. As settlers flooded west, they brought with them a restiveness and a rowdiness that became the stuff of legends. Due to the cheap, abundant supply of grain, alcohol abuse was rampant; water was deemed fine for navigation but not for consumption. People on the frontier—from infants to adults—drank before meals, during meals, and after meals, three meals a day. Spousal and child abuse followed. One in three brides was pregnant, attesting to the lack of religious presence on the frontier.[2]

Although Deism, Unitarianism, and Universalism had seeped south from New England, the migration of James McGready, a Scots-Irish Presbyterian preacher from North Carolina, to Logan County in August 1796 roughly coincided with the arrival of evangelical religion. McGready had enjoyed some revival success with his congregation in North Carolina, but no one could have predicted the thunderous revivals that ensued in the Cumberland Valley. Emboldened by a large camp-meeting gathering at Gaspar River during the last week of July 1800, several clergy began planning for another camp meeting at Cane Ridge the following summer.

By Saturday, August 9, 1801, somewhere between twelve thousand and twenty-five thousand settlers (estimates vary) had assembled at Cane Ridge, Kentucky, for a revival that has assumed almost mythic dimensions in American religious history. The camp meeting, which was an American adaptation of the Scottish tradition of "sacramental seasons," drew settlers from the surrounding region, and it was as much a social occasion as a religious revival. Although wags insisted that more souls were conceived than converted at camp-meeting revivals, the Cane Ridge gathering featured communal singing and sermons by preachers who had set aside the Calvinist doctrine of particular election in favor of the Arminian emphasis on free will.[3]

Those attending the camp meeting responded with conversions—and sometimes with spectacular spiritual manifestations. Contemporaries claimed that when people were overtaken by the Holy Spirit, they engaged in all sorts of bizarre behavior, ranging from involuntary contortions (called "the jerks") and ecstatic singing to falling down and the "barking exercise." The unfettered spiritual enthusiasm of the Great Revival provided a kind of nascent equality on the frontier: everyone, including women and slaves, was equal before God.[4]

Building on the momentum of Gaspar River and Cane Ridge, evangelicalism swept the South, leaving the unmistakable stamp of revivalism. Camp meetings became (and remain) an important fixture of religion in the South; B. W. Gorham even published a manual in 1854 explaining how to plan and carry off a successful camp meeting. Methodists and Baptists especially flourished on the frontier—Methodists because of their ingenious organization and their use of circuit riders, who brought religion to the people, and Baptists through a process somewhat akin to spontaneous generation. Rather than relying on clergy from the outside—the supply of ministers on the frontier usually fell short of the demand—many Baptists simply ordained one of their own. Baptists and Methodists also held an advantage over other denominations in the South, especially Presbyterians, because they did not require that their clergy be educated, and that circumstance, of course, shaped religion in the South. "In general, they have very little learning; though when they begin to preach, they begin to study, and many of them improve considerably," John Schermerhorn commented on Methodist preachers in 1814. "As to their manner of preaching, it very much resembles that of the Baptists—it is very controversial, and most bitter against Calvinists. They rail very much against the practice of Presbyterians' receiving pay for preaching, calling them hirelings, but most unreasonably; for their salaries are more certain and, in general, greater than those against whom they speak." The sermons that southerners heard—in the camp meeting, in the open fields, or from the pulpit—generally were based on the Bible alone and were marked by a kind of beguiling theological naïveté.[5]

If the Great Revival in the Cumberland Valley reshaped evangelical worship and created the evangelical culture in the South, the revival in western New York, the third theater of the Second Awakening, profoundly reshaped evangelical theology. The construction of the Erie Canal, completed in 1825, made western New York into a boom area. The canal opened markets in the East and triggered all manner of social, economic, and demographic changes; one minister in the area blamed the canal for bringing the "evils rolling through our land and among us." In the midst of this social upheaval, the revival fires swept through the region so frequently that it became known as the "Burned-Over District." Connecticut Congregationalist Lyman Beecher called the awakening in western New York "the greatest work of God, and the greatest revival of religion, that the world has ever seen." A number of religious and theological innovations arose in this environment—including the Church of Jesus Christ of Latter-day Saints, founded by Joseph Smith Jr. in 1830—but none was more significant than the "new measures" and the Arminian theology popularized by Charles Grandison Finney.[6]

Finney was trained as a lawyer, but he followed a call to the ministry and was ordained by the St. Lawrence Presbytery in 1824. Finney, ever the pragmatist, grew impatient with the Calvinist notion of election because he found it uncongenial to revivalism. Whereas Jonathan Edwards, apologist for the First Awakening, spoke of revival as "a surprising work of God," Finney insisted that revival was the work of man. Edwards, surveying the conversions everywhere around him in the late 1730s, remarked, "This seems to have been a very extraordinary dispensation of Providence:

God has in many respects gone out of, and much beyond his usual and ordinary way." Finney, however, saw things differently. "Religion is the work of man. It is something for man to do," he wrote. "It is not a miracle, or dependent on a miracle, in any sense. It is a purely philosophical result of the right use of the constituted means—as much so as any other effect produced by the application of means."[7]

Rather than wait for a visitation of the Holy Spirit, Finney taught that ministers could take matters into their own hands. He introduced a series of "new measures," including protracted revival meetings, the "anxious bench," and allowing women to exhort or testify, as surefire catalysts for revival. But his Arminian theology functioned on an individual level as well. Finney taught that sinners need not wait for some kind of "call" to conversion; instead, they could take matters into their own hands and initiate the process of salvation. Whereas Christian theologians from Augustine to Luther to Edwards had believed that the will was impaired by sin, Finney insisted that conversion was a simple matter of volition: choose good over evil, Jesus over Satan, heaven over hell.

Among a people who had only recently taken their *political* destiny into their own hands, Finney's message that Americans controlled their *spiritual* destinies as well was enormously attractive. The Calvinist notion of election, a staple of Puritan theology, became unpopular, and Calvinists themselves became objects of derision, witness Elias Smith's doggerel "On Predestination":

If all things succeed
Because they're decreed
And immutable impulses rule us;
Then praying and preaching,
And all such like teaching,
Is nought but a plan to fool us.

If destiny and fate,
Guide us this way and that,
As the coachman with bits guides his horses;

There's no man can stray,
But all go the right way,
As the stars in their different courses.

. . . .

Then with all he must pass
For a dull, senseless ass,
Who depends upon predestination.

Americans have long nurtured the illusion of self-determination; Arminianism enshrined that sentiment, and it also comported well with the rugged individualism that became the hallmark of American identity in the nineteenth century.[8]

If individuals were capable of perfection in the Arminian scheme, why not society itself? The Second Great Awakening unleashed a great deal of optimism about the possibility of establishing the millennial kingdom of God, as predicted in the book of Revelation. With the success of the revivals, the millennium, one thousand years of peace and righteousness, seemed well within reach. Believers could, by dint of their own efforts, bring about the kingdom of God here on earth—more specifically, here in America. "The wilderness shall bud and blossom as the rose before us; and we will not cease, till a Christian nation throws up its temples of worship on every hill and plain," Horace Bushnell declared to the American Home Missionary Society in 1847, "and the bands of a complete Christian commonwealth are seen to span the continent."[9]

This eschatology (theology of the end times) was postmillennialism, which held that Jesus would return to earth *after* the millennium. Postmillennialism implied that the millennium was attainable now, and postmillennial sentiments animated missionary efforts and most of the social reform movements and benevolent societies of the antebellum period. Evangelicals who believed that the millennium was at hand organized the temperance crusade, campaigns against dueling and other social vices, and advocated women's suffrage. They founded female seminaries and, most important, sought the abolition of slavery, the issue that would eventually drive a wedge between northern and southern evangelicals.

Postmillennialism had other effects as well. "We are all a little wild here with numberless projects of social reform," Ralph Waldo Emerson remarked in 1840. "Not a reading man but has a draft of a new community in his waist coat pocket." The conviction that the millennium was here or upon us inspired various utopian schemes and communitarian experiments, all trying to attain the perfected society. Mother Ann Lee and the Shakers believed that the millennium had arrived and that this circumstance demanded celibacy. John Humphrey Noyes, on the other hand, also believed that the millennium was here, but that conviction led him in precisely the opposite direction—to renounce the notion of exclusivity in marriage and to practice what he called "complex marriage" and, eventually, a program of genetic engineering he called "stirpiculture" in his Oneida Community. Other communities, such as Brook Farm, Fruitlands, and Bishop Hill, all imbibed postmillennial sentiments to one degree or another. When Adin Ballou inaugurated the Hopedale Community near Milford, Massachusetts, in 1842, for example, he urged residents to "inaugurate the kingdom of heaven on earth" and banish sin from the world.[10]

The postmillennial optimism of the antebellum period gave way to a growing sense of despair at midcentury. The carnage of the Civil War dimmed hopes for the impending millennium, and the rapid urbanization and industrialization of the postwar era did nothing to reverse that perception. The influx of non-Protestant immigrants, most of whom did not share evangelical scruples about temperance, further dampened expectations about the millennial kingdom. Late in the nineteenth century, teeming, squalid tenements, many of them burgeoning with labor unrest, hardly resembled the precincts of Zion so confidently predicted in the antebellum period.

In response, evangelicals shifted their theology from postmillennialism, the expectation that Jesus would return after the millennium, to premillennialism: Jesus will come at any moment, *before* the millennium. This "theology of despair" effectively exempted late nineteenth-century evangelicals from the task of social amelioration. Because Jesus would return imminently and rain down judgment against the ungodly, why worry about making the world a better place? Premillennialism stood in marked contrast to the postmillennial creed of antebellum Protestants, whose understanding of the Scriptures lent an urgency to their social-reform efforts.[11]

If Protestants, toiling beneath the constraints of postmillennialism, were planning for the future, they were also fixated with the past. For thousands of immigrants, beginning with the Pilgrims in 1620, America offered the chance to begin anew, to fashion something out of nothing without battling against stubborn institutions and centuries of ossified tradition. In the early republic, the impulse to begin anew was refracted through literalist readings of the Bible. Such readings, coupled with an impatience with tradition and denominational fissiparousness, very often issued in a primitivism among antebellum Protestants.[12]

Some groups, such as the Campbellites, the Christian Church, and the Disciples of Christ, enshrined this notion as the central part of their identity. "No creed but the Bible" became their creed, and they believed that they could replicate the primitive simplicity of New Testament Christianity. They sought to leapfrog nearly two thousand years of church history, thereby discarding all of the corrupting accretions of Roman Catholicism and other Protestants. They referred to themselves simply as "Christians."

Other groups—Mormons, Millerites, Landmark Baptists— also believed they could attain the primitive ideal, and they sought to define themselves solely by their understanding of the Bible. The widespread popular adoption of a simplified biblical hermeneutic at about the same time made their task even easier. Scottish Common Sense Realism, which became enormously influential among nineteenth-century evangelicals, was developed principally by Thomas Reid, a philosopher at the University of Glasgow, as a response to both the idealism of George Berkeley and the skepticism of David Hume. Scottish Realism (also known as Common Sense Realism) posited that ordinary people could gain a reliable grasp of the world though a responsible use of their senses. In addition to an apprehension of the physical world, the individual also possessed an innate "moral sense," which allowed for a grasp of foundational moral principles. In the realm of biblical interpretation, evangelicals used Common Sense Realism to argue that the meaning of the Scriptures was available to the faithful simply by reading the Bible and interpreting it in its plainest sense.

Scottish Realism was nothing if not democratic; everyone could appropriate the truths of the Bible, regardless of education or social standing. Although most antebellum Protestants failed to make the attribution, they had adopted wholesale Martin Luther's notion of the priesthood of believers; everyone was directly responsible before God for his or her salvation. Scottish Realism provided the faithful with the additional assurance that the meaning of the Bible was available to all in its plainest sense, and this conviction became an article of faith among antebellum Protestants, making the United States into a nation of theologians and biblical interpreters.

The Bible, an extraordinarily complex and apparently contradictory document, admits of many disparate interpretations—as illustrated throughout church history, and as amply demonstrated among antebellum Protestants. Abolitionists in the North read the New Testament as a radical manifesto for human freedom and equality, while Southern theologians interpreted the Bible as upholding the social order. Both camps even cited St. Paul, the apostle—Southerners Paul's letter to Philemon regarding Onesimus, and Northerners Paul's declaration to the Galatians: "There is neither Jew nor Greek, slave nor free, male nor female, for you are all one in Christ Jesus."[13]

Whereas American Protestants dating back to the Puritans liked to portray themselves as God's New Israel, fleeing religious persecution in the Old World for the Promised Land of toleration in the New World, African Americans, mired in slavery, read the story of ancient Israel through different eyes. They were God's chosen people wandering through the Egypt of slavery in search of the Promised Land of freedom.

These divergent interpretations of the same book, the same stories, constituted the basis for the nation's first truly moral crisis. Just as the political realm had to deal with the fundamental contradiction—the contradiction embodied in the person of Thomas Jefferson, statesman and slaveholder—between the horrors of slavery and the soaring republican rhetoric about "the rights of man" and "the pursuit of happiness" in America's charter documents, so too American Protestants were condemned to address the fundamental contradiction between servitude here on earth and freedom in Christ. This contradiction would expose fissures among America's Protestants—the Methodists split in 1844, the Baptists the following year, and the Presbyterians in 1857—and no one captured the dilemma of Protestant biblical interpretation better than Abraham Lincoln in his Second Inaugural Address. Both sides in this bitter war, the beleaguered president declared, prayed to the same God and read the same Bible.[14]

4

AN END TO UNJUST INEQUALITY IN THE WORLD
The Radical Tradition of Progressive Evangelicalism

In 1856 Methodist preacher Elijah H. Pilcher entertained an embarrassment of political options. Shortly after his conversion during a camp-meeting revival at age ten, Elijah Pilcher had resolved to enter the ministry. He assumed his first post, as a Methodist preacher on the Nicholas Circuit in southern Ohio, while still a teenager, preaching twenty-eight times a month. Assigned to the Ann Arbor Circuit at age twenty, Pilcher began his distinguished career in the territory of Michigan. As president of the board of trustees, in 1841 he laid the cornerstone for the first building of what would become Albion College, chartered as "The Wesleyan Seminary at Albion and Albion Female Collegiate Institute." The school admitted both sexes, but it paid particular attention in its early years to the education of women. A passionate advocate for public education, Pilcher agitated for the expansion and the enhancement of public schools in Romeo, Michigan, and he was appointed to the board of regents for the University of Michigan in 1845, a post he held until 1851. Pilcher signed on to the temperance movement in 1830; his only objection to the local Ann Arbor chapter was that they did not advocate total abstinence. On the contentious issue of slavery, Pilcher vigorously opposed the Fugitive Slave Law and, according to his son and biographer, "was always on the side of humanity and freedom." In 1852 he published a pamphlet titled "The Unconstitutionality of Slavery and the Fugitive Slave Law."[1]

As the election year of 1856 unfolded, the Abolition Party in Michigan nominated Pilcher to run for the position of superintendent of public instruction for the entire state. The Republican Party of Michigan proposed him for election as the state's superintendent of public schools, although he declined the nomination in favor of his friend. Completing the trifecta, the state's Democratic Party selected Pilcher for a seat on the state's board of education. Even though Pilcher declined all three nominations, the Democratic Party kept his name on the ticket, and the minister garnered more votes than any of the party's other nominees.[2]

Pilcher was hardly the only antebellum evangelical interested in political matters. "The gospel is adapted to promote the civil, social, and physical interests of man," S. H. Waldo, a minister in Dover, Ohio, declared in an address before the Society of Inquiry at Oberlin in 1849. "Civil government, where Christianity has its appropriate influence, is framed for the promotion of the universal good of the state, and not for the benefit of a few." Waldo was utterly confident that a proper apprehension of the gospel led to the assertion of female equality against the prevailing norms of society. "But let the religion of heaven throw its happy influence upon a given community, and a woman is raised from the dust, polished like the cornerstone of a palace, and placed as a companion by the side of man," he said. "The gospel is adapted to give our social nature *development*, *tone*, and *purity*."[3]

The evangelical mandate for remaking society in the early decades of the nineteenth century derived from a series of revivals that convulsed three theaters of the new nation: New England, the Cumberland Valley of Kentucky, and upstate New York, an area so frequently singed by the fires of revival that it became known as the Burned-Over District. These religious stirrings, known collectively as the Second Great Awakening, lured thousands of Americans into the ambit of evangelicalism. The evangelical camp-meeting revivals in the South were by far the most enthusiastic and dramatic. Settlers would gather for several days of preaching, prayer, and hymn-singing. Contemporaries spoke of all manner of religious ecstasy. Many of the auditors who succumbed to the influence of the Holy Spirit, whether voluntarily or not, were seized with various "exercises": shouting, barking, singing, falling down.

Revivals to the North tended to be more sedate but no less transformative. The epicenter of religious awakening in New England was Yale College, where Timothy Dwight, president of the school and grandson of the redoubtable Jonathan Edwards, succeeded in turning students away from Enlightenment Rationalism and toward orthodox Christianity. Writing to his mother on June 11, 1802, Benjamin Silliman, one of the students, described Yale as a "little temple" where "prayer and praise seem to be the delight of the greater part of the students." A correspondent for the *Connecticut Evangelical Magazine* sent details of another awakening at Yale in 1815, and Nathaniel William Taylor, then pastor of the First Congregational Church in New Haven, reported a more general revival in both the school and the town in January 1821. Even the Methodists took notice of the goings-on in New Haven, despite the fact that New England was hardly a stronghold of Methodism. A Yale student sent a dispatch to the Baltimore-based *Mutual Rights and Methodist Protestant* in 1831, noting that "the state of religion was so flourishing" during yet another revival taking place at the college "that it appeared as if the revival would go on as a matter of course."[4]

Due in no small measure to the agency of Yale graduates fanning across New England, newspapers began reporting revivals throughout the region, with datelines from such places as Troy and Cooperstown, New York; Woodbury and New Preston, Connecticut; Woodstock and Dorset and Bennington, Vermont; Bangor and Winthrop, Maine; Hanover and Portsmouth, New Hampshire; Pawtucket and Albion Mills, Rhode Island; Williamstown and Boston, Massachusetts. "We heartily rejoice in the conversion of sinners," an article titled "Glorious Intelligence from Vermont" recorded in the *Christian Intelligencer*. "From the smallest beginning," Wooster Parker reported from Castine, Maine, "and in spite of bitterest opposition, God is building up his church here." Methodists began to make inroads in New England. Presbyterians saw some success. Episcopal churches brought in new members. Baptists sent missionaries to organize Sunday schools and congregations in Vermont, Maine, and New Hampshire. "There has probably never been a time, when so many and so extensive revivals of religion existed in Connecticut, as at present," the *Missionary Herald* reported in 1821. "We rejoice that the light of the gospel of Christ is making its way through the mists of darkness that cover the earth," a Baptist periodical enthused.[5]

Abetted by the population and economic boom from construction of the Erie Canal, some of the revival energies shifted toward western New York by the late 1820s and early 1830s. "The state of religion is interesting here," a woman from Saratoga Springs wrote to a friend in Rochester, New York, in 1825. "There is great excitement, and a great degree of engagedness among Christians." Moses Rowley, an attorney, reported sixty-six baptisms at his church in Governeur, New York. "It really seems that the Lord is working wonders in this place," he wrote. "A new state of things exists," wrote Abiel Parmele, a minister from Forestville, New York, in Chautauqua County. "Protracted meetings have become abundantly multiplied, and no less abundantly blessed."[6]

The people of Rochester, New York, reported a "powerful revival of religion" as early as April 1827, but the real engine behind the awakening was Charles Grandison Finney, who arrived in the city in September 1830 to become pastor of the Third Presbyterian Church. Born in Warren, Connecticut, in 1792 and trained as a lawyer, Finney had an evangelical conversion in 1821 that utterly changed his life and altered the course of history. Scheduled to argue a case in court the day following his conversion, Finney informed his startled client, "I have a retainer from the Lord Jesus Christ to plead his cause, and I cannot plead yours." Following his ordination as a Presbyterian minister in 1824, Finney embarked on a career as a revivalist and later as a professor and president of Oberlin College.[7]

It was in Rochester, however, that Finney burst onto the national scene. "Mr. Finney is preaching to overflowing houses," the readers of the *Baptist Chronicle* learned in December 1830. "Conversions are daily occurring," including "men of wealth, talents, and influence." By the following spring, and due in part to Finney's innovative evangelistic strategies, Rochester was consumed by revival. "It has by all accounts been a work of great power and of unusual efficiency," the *Rhode Island Journal* reported on May 27, 1831, adding that "a goodly number of friends of religion anticipate a reviving scene far beyond what they have thus far witnessed." A writer in the *Morning Star* suggested that, "Of all the favored spots of our highly favored land, none, perhaps, have shared more largely than Rochester, in the outpouring of the Spirit." African Americans also responded to revival preaching. Two "respectable African preachers" arrived in town, one from Pennsylvania and the other from Ontario, according to the *African Repository & Colonial Journal*, and their efforts produced such an evangelical awakening "the like has never been known among the Africans in this place before!"[8]

Finney, however, together with other leaders of the Second Great Awakening, believed that evangelicalism entailed more than mere conversions. A regenerated individual, in obedience to the teachings of Jesus, bore responsibility for the improvement of society and especially the interests of those most vulnerable. Finney, in fact, understood benevolence toward others as a necessary corollary of faith. "God's rule requires universal benevolence," he wrote. "I abhor a piety which has no humanity with it and in it," he added. "God loves both piety and humanity."[9]

A writer in *Christian Reformer,* published out of Harrisburg, Pennsylvania, recognized that the believers' mandate for reform came from the exemplar of the "true spirit of benevolence," Jesus himself. "But, however we may be looked upon by the world," he wrote, "let us never forget that we are disciples of a reformer, the most thorough reformer, the most zealous reformer, the most courageous reformer that mankind ever saw." The task of the believer, therefore, was nothing less than reform of society. "The general principles of Christianity, as well as the example of its founder, impel us to take part in every reformation," he continued, "every man is bound, by his responsibility to God, to promote the best interests of his fellow creatures."[10]

The initial decades of the nineteenth century witnessed an effusion of voluntary associations dedicated to social welfare, and the unmistakable catalyst for such groups was religion. Finney and other antebellum evangelicals envisioned nothing less than a benevolent empire. "Now the great business of the church is to reform the world," Finney wrote. "The church of Christ was originally organized to be a body of reformers. The very profession of Christianity implies the profession and virtually an oath to do all that can be done for the universal reformation of the world." An article in the *Religious Monitor & Evangelical Repository* concurred, noting that "the sentiment is rapidly gaining ground in all parts of the country, that the *church* is the divinely appointed *means* of producing moral and religious reforms." Finney understood this initiative as a battle against sin, and he especially applauded the work that evangelical women had undertaken in this struggle, even as he castigated his fellow clergy for their apathy: "It is amazing to see what excuses are made by ministers for remaining silent in respect to almost every branch of reform."[11]

Evangelicals in the antebellum period insisted on the necessity of benevolence. "Mercy is that affection of the mind, by which we feel the distresses of our fellow-creatures, and become disposed to assist and relieve them," an article in the *Piscataqua Evangelical Magazine* began. A benevolent person "will not say to a brother or sister who is naked and destitute of food, depart in peace, be thou warmed and filled, and, at the same time, give them not those things that are needful to the body." An article in the *Christian Examiner and Theological Review* pointed out the "inseparable connexion between faith and works" and the "utter worthlessness of all that faith, which terminates in speculation." Other evangelicals believed that benevolence would prove to be the core of national identity. "The spirit of nationality will not depend, for its nourishment, upon the mad spirit of war, nor even upon the ties of worldly interest," a writer in the *Christian Spectator* opined. "It will be maintained by a principle stronger than death, and more perpetual than the sun: union in the cause of benevolence."[12]

Benevolence took many forms, including education, prison reform, and advocacy for the poor and for the rights of women. Many evangelicals, seeking to obey the commands of Jesus to love their enemies and turn the other cheek, enlisted in efforts to oppose war. Still others, including Finney, took a dim view of capitalism and business practices. Even though the evangelical obsession with temperance looks presumptuous and paternalistic in hindsight, the temperance movement was a response to the very real depredations and suffering, including child and spousal abuse, caused by excessive alcohol consumption.[13]

Antebellum evangelicals, like Elijah Pilcher of Michigan, saw universal public education as a means of advancing the fortunes of those less privileged. "Common Schools are the glory of our land," a writer declared in the *Christian Spectator*, "where even the beggar's child is taught to read, and write, and think, for himself."[14]

Joshua Leavitt, a Congregational minister in Stratford, Connecticut, who would go on to be one of the era's most passionate abolitionists, produced two editions of *Easy Lessons in Reading* for use in common schools. "A competent degree of education pervades all classes of people," a writer in the *Quarterly Christian Spectator* declared. "This state of things will not be questioned, as presenting a peculiar means and medium of achieving much in the cause of benevolence." A true person of faith, he added, "carries his love of knowledge with him" and "regularly erects a school-house by the side of the altar."[15]

Sabbath schools initially taught the rudiments of literacy, especially to the children one evangelical proponent described as "the victims of ignorance and wretchedness." Only with the advent of common schools did Sabbath (or Sunday) schools redefine themselves. "The teaching of children to read and write on the Sabbath," an article in the *Boston Recorder* noted in 1818, "is a branch of the general system that may properly be dispensed with, in every place where children are universally taught to read and write, on other days." Sabbath schools shifted to religious instruction, but the general effect was "almost miraculous success in improving the character and condition of the poor." A correspondent writing in the *Christian Spectator* could think of no comparable institution "which actually engages in the divine work of gratuitously doing good to others, so many hands and hearts, or exerts so wide and efficacious an influence, at once to relieve the miseries, and amend the characters, of the ignorant and the vicious."[16]

Evangelicals well understood the target of their efforts, especially in the cities: "children of the extremely indigent" and "people of colour." In 1826 the American Board of Commissioners for Foreign Missions reported its educational activities among Native Americans. Among the Cherokees "there are upwards of two hundred children receiving the benefits of a common education," the board reported. "So diligent are the pupils, that at a recent examination of one of the schools, in no instance was a single word of the spelling lessons incorrectly given." Educational efforts among Native Americans often suppressed their traditions in coercive ways, underscoring what theologians refer to as the ambiguity of all human effort; but for many evangelicals, the formation of Sabbath schools had opened their eyes to the plight of others. "At the first proposal for their establishment, the public were but very imperfectly aware of the numbers, among the lower classes, whom they could greatly benefit," one of the organizers recalled. But the search for students "led to a discovery of the real condition of the poor, and astonished even the advocates of the institution, by developing the great number of the illiterate, to whom it might afford the greatest assistance."[17]

Evangelicals also set their sights on higher education. "If a more general diffusion of knowledge, and indeed a deeper tincture in those who possess it, be necessary to the cause of christianity [*sic*], it is equally so for the moral and political improvement of society," a writer in the *Virginia Evangelical & Literary Magazine* began. He complained that "even the domestic education of youth is entirely too careless and superficial." The writer, who described himself as a "Provincial Protestant," called for a national commitment to higher learning: "We should, if possible, procure celebrated professors for our universities, whose genius and renown would shed lustre upon letters, whose eloquence would impart warmth and grace to whatever it touched, whose imaginations could conjure up and paint before their pupils all the touching images which hallowed the schools of antiquity." America, this evangelical believed, would soon eclipse Europe in intellectual attainments. "Let the genius of American science unscale its eagle eye," he wrote, "gaze upon, and soar to the fountain of heavenly radiance, and animated by grateful remembrances of her European progenitors, visit and comfort her aged parent when she shall be forsaken in her old age." Evangelicals also sought to make higher education available to those of lesser means. An article in the *Evangelical Monitor*, published out of Woodstock, Vermont, praised the extensive efforts by the president and trustees of Amherst College to assist lower-income students. "It was the original design of this institution to furnish an education for the charity students *at a cheap rate*," the publication noted approvingly.[18]

Political and social concerns, especially those directed toward the less fortunate in society, spill out of the pages of evangelical publications. "Let then the noble work of charity and kindness to the suffering poor go forward," a Methodist from Pittsburgh declared. Ebenezer Elliot published some doggerel in the pages of the *Evangelical Magazine and Gospel Advocate*:

> Wrong not the laboring poor by whom you live!
> Wrong not your humble fellow-worms, ye proud!
> For God will not the poor man's wrongs forgive,
> But hear his plea, and have his plea allowed.

A Methodist minister, writing in the *Western Christian Advocate*, told of a recent journey from Kentucky to Tuscaloosa, Alabama, to attend a church gathering. He encountered a poor woman walking with her children along a road, "surrounded with almost every consideration of earthly horror; in a lone wilderness, without a penny or an earthly friend, too feeble and debilitated by sickness and hunger to attempt greater speed than she was then making." The minister and his companion gave the woman all the money they had. When they arrived at their destination, "I felt that I was almost cursed with money, and longed for an opportunity to give it to the Lord or to some of his representatives, *the poor*."[19]

The early efforts of the Prison Discipline Society received plaudits from the evangelical newspaper *Zion's Herald*. "Not until the present time, has the cheering prospect been presented to Christian philanthropy of an association of gentlemen, standing high in the estimation of the public, combined for the avowed purpose of searching out and remedying the abuses of prison discipline," the *Herald* wrote. "We say God speed to those benevolent gentlemen whose united efforts are thus directed to purify the penitentiary system, as pursued in the United States, of many glaring fundamental errors." The editors of the *Virginia Evangelical & Literary Magazine* declared themselves "warm advocates of the Penitentiary system." While fear of punishment had its place in deterring crime, "it is impossible to bring a man to repentance by fear alone; its legitimate fruit is despair." The editors believed that "in the conduct of a Penitentiary, tenderness, and compassion must be mingled with severity; and hope must diffuse its stimulating and cheering influences through the whole man."[20]

For James H. Fairchild, an ordained minister and professor of mathematics and natural philosophy at Oberlin College, the matter of gender equality was self-evident. To the question "What are woman's rights and duties?" Fairchild replied, "The same, in general as those of all other human beings, because she possesses the common attributes of humanity." Although Fairchild could not shake essentialist assumptions about men and women, and he was not yet prepared to extend women the right to vote, he nevertheless argued for equality of wages for equal work. "The laborer is worthy of his hire," he said, "and it is desirable that woman should receive according to the work she does."[21]

C. C. Foote, of Farmington, Michigan, thought that Fairchild's argument for female equality did not go far enough. In the fascicle of the *Oberlin Quarterly Review* that followed the one printing of Fairchild's lecture, Foote argued that the issue of gender equality would not be settled "until woman takes her rightful place *beside* (not beneath) her equal brother man." Foote, a minister, argued from Scripture for the ordination of women. He called for the extension of suffrage to women, linking the absence of such rights to the denial of rights to African Americans. "One is forcibly reminded of the logic by which our colored brother is denied his rights," he wrote.[22]

"We maintain that women are not inferior to men," the *Literary and Evangelical Magazine*, published in Richmond, declared in 1828. An article titled "The Mental Capacities of the Sexes Considered" in the *Evangelical Magazine and Gospel Advocate* called attention to the social advantages enjoyed by men. "When gentlemen are at school, they are provided with separate rooms, commodious playgrounds, large and well selected libraries, philosophical, chemical, and astronomical apparatus," the writer noted, "lectures on almost every subject, and what is better than all, are allowed to freely express their minds without the *charge* of *pedantry*." Women, by contrast, must pursue their learning "with one little innocent in her arm, rocking another in the cradle, while one more is at her elbow asking for bread and butter, and, at the same time, the oldest ones [*sic*] knitting work must be fixed!" Level the playing field, the author suggested, and see "if she does not give evidence of so great intellectual power."[23]

The editor of *Zion's Herald*, one of the most influential evangelical publications during the antebellum period, introduced his newspaper to the evangelical world on January 9, 1823. "No period, since the establishment of Christianity," he wrote, "has manifested such a spirit of inquiry among Christians as the present." While he sought to steer clear of political topics, he nevertheless thought it important to articulate the bedrock principles of political evangelicalism: "The Editor, notwithstanding he disclaims party politics, considers it his duty, as a christian [*sic*] and citizen, to inculcate the principles of freedom and equal rights."[24]

Other evangelicals, by contrast, were unabashedly partisan. Elias Smith of Portsmouth, New Hampshire, a crusader for religious disestablishment, was clear about the shape of his politics. He regarded the one-term presidency of John Adams, a Federalist, as "a four years scourge to the United States," whereas Adams' successor, Thomas Jefferson, "was raised up by the King of kings, to fill the most important place in the world." Smith believed that Christianity "as explained in the New Testament, is calculated to level all distinctions among men that are not founded upon intrinsic merit." In his *Herald of Gospel Liberty*, Smith expressed confidence that evangelical sentiments would transform believers from Federalists to Jeffersonian Republicans. "Almost all who are converted to the Lord, are Republicans," he observed. "Why is this so? Because converts are redeemed with righteousness; and of course are right in things political as well as things religious." Elsewhere, endorsing a candidate for governor of New Hampshire as "a man of the People," Smith concluded his appeal with a kind of benediction: "My heart's desire is, that my enemies may be converted to God, and the truth; become honest Republicans, real Christians, have peace in their own souls, be a blessing to the world, live happy, die blessed, and enjoy the reward of Grace in a world without end."[25]

Elias Smith did not speak for all northern evangelicals. Except for Methodists and Baptists—outsiders—most evangelicals in the North viewed Jefferson with suspicion, and so they were unlikely to rally behind a rabble-rouser like Smith. But Elias Smith was not alone in believing that the teachings of Jesus betrayed a preference for the poor. "Multitudes of the poor love the name and religion of Jesus Christ," he wrote. "There is no doubt but that God regards all his creatures; but yet from motives of mercy and compassion, there is an evident predilection for the *poor*, manifested in our Saviour's preaching and ministry." Smith believed that "the middle ranks and the poor, that is, the great majority of mankind, should place a due value in the gospel, not only for its religious, but also for its civil and political advantages." Jesus Christ, Smith believed, "came to put an end to unjust inequality in the world."[26]

Despite Finney's criticism of clergy, many evangelical ministers were hardly silent in the antebellum period. After Josiah Bushnell Grinnell preached an antislavery sermon in 1852, he lost his job as pastor of First Congregational Church in Washington, D.C. "My mother took a high view of religious studies," Grinnell recalled. On pain of missed suppers, she demanded that her children memorize a verse of Scripture every day. After a stint in Wisconsin as agent for the American Tract Society, Grinnell enrolled at Auburn Theological Seminary. His first church, in Union, just outside of Albany, New York, was biracial, and the congregation doubled during his brief tenure. Grinnell's church in the nation's capital attracted members of Congress to its pews. After being run out of Washington for his antislavery sentiments, Grinnell briefly spent time in New York City, where he made the acquaintance of Horace Greeley.[27]

It was to Grinnell that Greeley, editor of the *New-York Tribune*, issued his famous admonition, "Go West, young man, go West!" Grinnell heeded the advice, working briefly as a reporter for Greeley's *Tribune*, covering the 1853 Illinois State Fair. Writing in both the *Tribune* and another publication, the *New York Independent*, Grinnell summoned utopian adventurers "desirous of educational facilities, and of temperance and Congregational affinities," to help him build a town where church and school would be central. Several responded, including a physician from Maine; they gathered in March 1854 to construct such a "broad, generous and beneficent" town. Five years later, Iowa College, subsequently renamed in honor of its founder, opened its doors. When Greeley visited Grinnell, Iowa, later in life, he pronounced the town a model city in both morals and education. The pulpit of the Congregational church in Grinnell hosted an array of luminaries, including Elizabeth Cady Stanton, Lucy Stone, and Dwight L. Moody.[28]

Grinnell's religious convictions informed his politics. He won election to the state senate in 1856 on a platform of temperance, free soil, and universal education. In 1858 he shepherded a free-school bill through the legislature. Grinnell deplored nativism, advocated women's rights, admired the evangelical philanthropists Arthur and Lewis Tappan, and made his town a stop on the Underground Railroad. In 1859 John Brown stopped by with several escaped slaves on his way back east from his antislavery agitations in Kansas. Brown planned his raid on Harper's Ferry while in Grinnell, which made Grinnell himself a suspect as coconspirator, though he was never indicted. In 1863 Grinnell returned to Washington, this time as a member of Congress for two terms.[29]

Many evangelical sentiments in the antebellum period would be considered radical by the standards of both the twentieth and twenty-first centuries. Finney's understanding of the Christian faith and duty led him to a suspicion of capitalism because it was suffused with avarice and selfishness, a critique shared by many Roman Catholics as well. Finney allowed that "the business aims and practices of business men are almost universally an abomination in the sight of God." What are the principles of those who engage in business? Finney asked. "Seeking their own ends; doing something not for others, but for self." Finney enumerated "another thing which is highly esteemed among men, yet is an abomination before God," namely "selfish ambition."[30]

Elsewhere, Finney preached even more explicitly against the mores of business. "The whole course of business in the world is governed and regulated by the maxims of supreme and unmixed selfishness," Finney said. "The maxims of business generally current among business men, and the habits and usages of business men, are all based upon supreme selfishness." Finney indicted capitalism itself, arguing that the "whole system recognizes only the love of self" and "the rules by which business is done in the world, are directly opposite to the gospel of Jesus Christ, and the spirit he exhibited." The man of business, by contrast, lives by the maxim "Look out for number one."[31]

A writer in the *New-York Evangelist* echoed Finney's concerns, suggesting that the integrity of the church itself had been compromised by its associations with the world of business. "The prosperity of the times in the business world threatens to endanger the piety of the church," he wrote, adding that businessmen were already insinuating their principles in the nation's pulpits. "The desire to possess, though constitutional, is one of the most dangerous affections of the human heart," he warned. "Can the heart be sanctified by constant contact with goods and merchandize, bills and invoices, notes and monies, checks and drafts?" These accoutrements of business threatened the very souls of believers. "In devising as well as prosecuting their schemes of money-making, American Christians find themselves associated, if not identified with the most devoted servants of mammon, the world can afford." The author cited, in particular, the pernicious influence of "The Chambers of Commerce" and lamented that the "bias of heart toward money-making, has become an American characteristic."[32]

An evangelical farmer, writing from Vermont in 1837, offered corroboration, citing the deleterious effects of "wild speculations, arising from an undue anxiety to be hastily rich." An article in the *New-York Evangelist* similarly took a dim view of acquisitive wealth, arguing "that the believer who devotes all that is given him beyond his present necessities to the cause of Christian benevolence, trusting God for the supply of his future wants, acts more according to the mind of Christ, than he who treasures up of his abundance as a future provision for himself or family." The *Christian Chronicle* expressed similar reservations. "Riches, alas! are often amassed by the arts of oppression, extortion and deceit," the article warned. "Thus acquired, the blessing of heaven cannot rest upon them."[33]

A writer in the *Virginia Evangelical & Literary Magazine* asserted that America was a place where "talent and merit" were superior to "unmerited and often ill gotten riches." "Whatever tends to consolidate wealth in the hands of a few," he said, "is manifestly contrary to the genius of our government." Another writer in the *Quarterly Christian Spectator*, published by Yale Divinity School, argued that the relative wealth of the United States conferred an obligation to those less fortunate. "When these things are considered, what conclusion can be drawn, but that the citizens of this nation should do good with their superabundance?" he asked. "With their essential wealth as a community, they may, and they ought to do, *much good*," he wrote; "a helping hand might be effectually extended to the destitute of other communities."[34]

The *Virginia Evangelical & Literary Magazine* addressed the issue of usury in 1819, concluding that "the custom of making money by exacting usurious interest is unfriendly to morals, and utterly destructive of the best feeling of the human heart." Instead, the writers expressed confidence that "the individual who is content with the slow and regular gains of patient and persevering industry, and is satisfied with plain and frugal fare, enjoys more real pleasure than the *speculator* and *shaver* who succeed in their schemes, and riot on their ill gotten wealth." A subsequent article in the same publication advanced the argument that economic stringency was good for spiritual well-being. The current financial climate would "probably make men more moral, in many respects" by encouraging frugality and prompting them to "deal less in speculation and credit."[35]

Violence in society was very much a concern for antebellum evangelicals. An article in the *Western Christian Advocate* inveighed against "the serious and gross impropriety of carrying arms," which it deemed "ungentlemanly, ruffian-like, cowardly and dangerous." *Zion's Herald* took aim at dueling. After writing about what the publication considered an especially egregious duel in 1838, the paper asked, "Shall it be left to the *press* alone, to arouse the moral sense of the community to a suitable detestation of this savage practice?" The *Herald* called on preachers to sound the alarm, to "utter their solemn protest, not only against the inhuman practice itself, but against every thing calculated either directly or indirectly to sustain it." When the U.S. Senate passed antidueling legislation later that year, the *Herald* declared, "We rejoice at the passage of this bill."[36]

A group of evangelicals organized the New-York Peace Society in 1815. "The Society originated with a few individuals," the organization's annual report recalled three years later, "from the conviction that war is inconsistent with the Christian religion, immoral in its acts, and repugnant to the true interests of mankind." Members of the society worked toward the day when "these sentiments would become universal" and "men would beat their swords into ploughshares, and their spears into pruning hooks, and learn war no more." The Vermont Peace Society opened its membership to "Any person of good moral character, who receives the Bible as the rule of his faith."[37]

Henry Clarke Wright, an alumnus of Andover Theological Seminary and a Congregational minister in West Newbury, Massachusetts, provides yet another example of antebellum evangelical sentiment. Wright, who had an evangelical conversion in the Burned-Over District of western New York, opposed slavery and was a feminist. He supported temperance and Christian education. But he also became increasingly sensitive to expressions of violence. While working as an agent for the American Sunday School Union, Wright denounced the corporal punishment of children. "The first principle of all education," he declared, "should be to direct the affections to God, to restrain the passions and form the appetites and habits on Christian principles."[38]

By 1833, after attending a gathering of the American Peace Society, Wright resolved to "pray more for peace and preach much more about it." After a brief stint as agent for the American Peace Society, Wright joined William Lloyd Garrison as one of the founders of the New England Non-Resistance Society in 1838. "We cannot acknowledge allegiance to any human government," the new organization's "Declaration of Principles" read. "We register our testimony, not only against all war, but against all preparation for war." The society's newspaper, the *Non-Resistant*, carried the motto "Resist Not Evil—Jesus Christ." Consistent with the principles of evangelical feminism, the new organization appointed several women to its executive committee.[39]

A series of articles in the *New-York Evangelist* also questioned the morality of war. "It does not appear that any Christian nation was ever, even temporarily, benefited by an engagement in war," the author began. Even the American Revolution might not have been justified, despite Americans' grandiose claims of "greater Christianity, liberty and equality." Those sentiments rang hollow, the author said, considering that the United States, in its brief history, "had accumulated so much of the guilt of oppression and inhumanity as this so soon, considering its treatment towards the red and black races." The author believed that the violence rampant in society—dueling, murders, and suicides—could be attributed, at least in part, to "the shedding of so much blood in war," which "hardened the human heart." War was fundamentally antithetical to the Christian faith, he insisted. "The spirit of the gospel or New Testament, throughout, is understood to be diametrically opposed to the spirit of war."[40]

Thomas C. Upham, graduate of Dartmouth College and Andover Theological Seminary, added his voice to the peace movement. Through its "moral influence, by the power of argument and persuasion alone," he wrote in 1840, the United States, in cooperation with other nations, had the opportunity to secure "the perpetual abolition of private war upon the ocean." Upham, a professor at Bowdoin College and a Congregational minister who had been swept up in the holiness movement a year earlier, advocated for a "Congress of Nations" that would adjudicate treaties, provide humanitarian aid, eradicate the "great evil" of the slave trade, and regulate the conduct of war, if not eliminate it altogether. Upham called for demilitarization on an international scale, decrying the "immense sums, applied to the slaughter of the human race" that might better be "expended in the culture of the earth, in purposes of commerce, in feeding the hungry, and clothing the naked, and healing the sick, and in various ways diminishing the aggregate of misery and increasing the sum of happiness."[41]

Upham sought nothing less, however, than the "entire and permanent extinction of war." This would be the great work of any such

Congress of Nations. "Wars must end," Upham declared, because "they are obviously opposed to the spirit and letter of the gospel; that religion and benevolence and the common sympathies and wants of humanity all cry aloud for their permanent termination."[42]

The editors of the *New-York Evangelist* explicitly linked the cessation of wars to the millennial kingdom. The paper listed a series of "peace measures," including "Urge universally on individuals and nations the claims of justice" and "Advocate the adoption of the principle of referring national disputes to the arbitration of neutral and friendly powers." If these measures were combined with the principles of truth and justice, the editors wrote, "we verily believe the millenial [sic] age will be introduced and maintained."[43]

Paradoxically, the aversion of evangelicals in the North toward the scourge of slavery would lead the nation inexorably toward the expression of violence that many evangelicals found repugnant. William B. Brown, a minister in Sandusky, Ohio, opined that "the inmates of our penitentiaries" were, "as a class, gentlemen, benefactors to the world, and almost saints before God, in comparison with the great mass of slave-holders at the south, and many of their abettors at the north."[44]

Finney and other evangelicals believed that the evangelical notion of benevolence was germane to the contemporary debates over slavery. "Perfect love never overreaches, nor defrauds, nor does any ill to a neighbor," he wrote. "Would a man that loved God with all his heart, perfectly, hold his neighbor as a slave?" he asked. Never. "There cannot be greater falsehood and hypocrisy," Finney declared, "than for a man who will do that, to pretend that he loves God." C. W. Gardner, pastor of the First Colored Presbyterian Church in Philadelphia, declared that "slavery was a system of robbery of the slave" for the simple reason that "it takes from him his rights."[45]

Even Southern evangelicals understood the enormity of slavery, although they differed from Northern evangelicals on how to end it. A writer in the *Virginia Evangelical & Literary Magazine* acknowledged slavery as "the greatest political evil which has ever entered the United States" and the slave trade as an "object of general detestation." But, like other Southerners, he dismissed the notion of outright abolition. He commended instead the work of the American Colonization Society as the "brightest beam of hope which has ever arisen on this dark subject." He encouraged his readers to "patronize this society and facilitate its operations as much as possible; and in the mean time, let us give the slaves such instruction as may qualify them for forming a prosperous colony." A writer from North Carolina sent a dispatch to the editor of the *Evangelical Witness* with a similar suspicion of abolition, even as he acknowledged that "the intelligent part of the southern section of the United States, have long regarded slavery both as a moral and political evil, as it exists in our country."[46]

The rhetoric over slavery built toward a crescendo in the 1840s and 1850s as the nation drifted toward war, but one of the overriding characteristics of evangelical arguments against slavery was not so much a desire to perpetuate the Union as it was a concern for slaves and slave families themselves. "Nothing can be more humiliating to human nature, or more offensive in the sight of a just God," Thomas Upham wrote in 1840, "than the fact that, multitudes of our fellow-beings are, from year to year, causelessly and violently torn away from their homes and friends, and consigned to hopeless servitude in foreign lands." Upham appealed to the shared humanity between whites and blacks. "Look round upon your own family, and put the question to your own heart," he urged, "and then say, whether the cruel treatment of African fathers and African children is a trifling concern."[47]

The reforming impulses of evangelicalism in the North, especially opposition to slavery, finally drove an angry South to secession. By the time Confederate guns blazed against Fort Sumter in the early morning hours of April 12, 1861, evangelical piety in the South had turned inward, while evangelicalism north of the Mason-Dixon line held out for a benevolent empire that encompassed virtually all elements of life, from personal morality to public policy, from individual comportment to economic systems and international relations. The vision of society articulated by Charles Finney and other evangelicals took special notice of those on the margins of society—women, slaves, the victims of war and abuse, prisoners, the poor—those Jesus called "the least of these."

The vision of nineteenth-century evangelicalism stands in marked contrast to the political agenda of the majority of evangelicals at the turn of the twenty-first century. To be sure, some evangelicals in the earlier era took a dim view of social reform, either because of contrary political leanings or because they feared that it diverted attention from evangelism. But in contrast to the predilections of evangelicals late in the twentieth century, the dominant nineteenth-century agenda was reformist, directed toward the benefit of those on the margins. Whereas antebellum evangelicals supported common schools as a democratizing influence and a vehicle of upward mobility for those less fortunate, many contemporary evangelicals decry public education and seek taxpayer support for sectarian schools. Evangelicals worked for the cessation of wars in the early decades of the nineteenth century, whereas evangelicals early in the twenty-first century overwhelmingly supported the invasion of both Iraq and Afghanistan. Nineteenth-century evangelicals advocated equal rights for women, but many evangelicals late in the twentieth century resisted the proposed Equal Rights Amendment to the Constitution. At the turn of the twenty-first century, politicians with evangelical sympathies regularly tout their pro-business and free enterprise credentials. Many—possibly most—evangelicals of an earlier age, however, criticized "the rules by which business is done in the world" as "directly opposite to the gospel of Jesus Christ."[48]

Although few evangelicals could have suspected it at the time, the evangelical benevolent empire had reached its apotheosis by 1860. With the onset of the Civil War, the shining aspirations of evangelical social amelioration began to dim for several decades as Americans coped with the devastation of the war and addressed the delicate task of mending the torn fabric of the republic. Even then, however, evangelicals were active in various freedman's associations, seeking to provide education and integration of African Americans into American life. In the waning decades of the nineteenth century, evangelical benevolence shifted toward the newly burgeoning cities with their roiling labor unrest and teeming, squalid tenements. Many evangelicals joined with more theologically liberal Protestants in a movement known as Social Christianity, or the Social Gospel, which held that Jesus is capable of redeeming not only sinful individuals but sinful social institutions as well. They organized "slum brigades" and rescue missions and recreational opportunities, but they also sought to reform the systemic abuses that lay behind human misery. Advocates of the Social Gospel worked hand in hand with political progressives on behalf of child-labor laws, housing reform, and the six-day workweek. They battled against alcohol abuse and corrupt political machines.

Indeed, intemperate alcohol consumption continued to be a social problem, and no one addressed this concern more single-mindedly than Frances Willard, who spent much of her childhood attending Charles Finney's church in Oberlin, Ohio. A Methodist and a graduate of Northwestern Female College in Evanston, Illinois, Willard had been nominated by the Illinois Republican Party in 1874—at a time when women were not allowed to vote—for state superintendent of public instruction. Despite losing the election, Willard continued her fight against the depredations of alcohol abuse, becoming president of the Woman's Christian Temperance Union in 1881, which, in addition to temperance, worked to shelter prostitutes, support labor unions for women, and improve prison conditions. "The Bible is the most political of books," Willard declared to the organization's national convention in 1887, emphasizing the mandate for social reform. She also pressed her advocacy for women. "I firmly believe God has a work for them to do as evangelists," she said, "as bearers of Christ's message to the ungospeled, to the prayer meeting, to the church generally and to the world at large." Willard, who participated in meetings of the National Woman Suffrage Association, counted Susan B. Anthony among her friends. Willard's activism inspired other evangelical women, including many in the South.[49]

Although William Jennings Bryan, the "Great Commoner" from Nebraska, is generally remembered for his bumbling performance at the Scopes Trial in Dayton, Tennessee, in 1925, he enjoyed a long career as an evangelical reformer. Bryan, three-time Democratic nominee for president, was a tireless advocate for the working and middle classes. He advocated taxing the rich, subsidizing farmers, and legislating against the abuses of unbridled capitalism. In his most famous speech, at the 1896 Democratic National Convention, Bryan employed biblical metaphors to press his case in favor of silver money, which would benefit the lower classes, against the privileged elite. "Having behind us the commercial interests and the laboring interests and all the toiling masses, we shall answer their demands for a gold standard by saying to them, you shall not press down upon the brow of labor this crown of thorns," Bryan thundered. "You shall not crucify mankind upon a cross of gold." Bryan's faith informed his activism. "When you hear a good democratic speech it is so much like a sermon that you can hardly tell the difference between them," he said in 1904. Bryan resigned as Woodrow Wilson's secretary of state in 1915 because of his disagreement with Wilson's decision to enter World War I.[50]

Aimee Semple McPherson, the firebrand pentecostal preacher and founder of the International Church of the Foursquare Gospel, regarded Franklin Roosevelt's New Deal as a "godsend" to pull desperate Americans out of the mire of the Great Depression. McPherson's Angelus Temple, in the Echo Park neighborhood of Los Angeles, was a hub of social activism, caring for the indigent and taking in unwed mothers. Decades later, Roberta Salter, McPherson's daughter, recalled teenage girls lingering in the narthex of Angelus Temple, waiting to talk with the famous evangelist. "She'd put her arm around their shoulders and say, 'Come on, are you hungry? Let's go over to the parsonage,'" Salter said. "She'd walk them over to the parsonage door and yell into the kitchen, 'Another place at the table!' Then she sat down with the girl and said, 'Tell me about it.'" McPherson was also an advocate for temperance, for the elderly, for the poor, and for workers' rights. She devoted one sermon to a comparison of gangsters with the barons of capitalism, suggesting that Al Capone's money, "although obtained by unscrupulous methods, is no more unclean than the dollars of the man who amasses his millions from underpaid factory workers."[51]

The roll call of progressive evangelicalism thins out in the decades following the 1920s; evangelicals by and large turned inward in these years, directing their considerable energies toward the construction of the evangelical subculture, a vast and interlocking network of congregations, Bible institutes, seminaries, camps, missionary societies, and publishing houses. Those evangelicals who did engage in politics tilted toward the right: John Brown, Robert "Fighting Bob" Shuler, J. Vernon McGee, George Pepperdine, Carl McIntire, and others.[52]

By the 1960s and early 1970s, progressive evangelicals looking for political role models cast a wider net, setting their sights on such figures as George McGovern, Democratic senator from South Dakota and son of a Wesleyan Methodist minister. McGovern, a prairie populist, also claimed the mantle of the Social Gospel. "But don't forget that that includes the word 'gospel' as well as 'social,'" he reminded an interviewer in the 1990s. "I believe in the teachings of Christ that the central commandment is to love God and to love our neighbors." Affirming his belief in the resurrection of Jesus, McGovern added, "It's always wrong, in my opinion, to exploit somebody else's labor unfairly, to make people work for wages that are an insult to human dignity, or to make them work under conditions that are unnecessarily dangerous."[53]

In the early 1970s, and especially during McGovern's run for the presidency in 1972, many evangelicals questioned whether or not the South Dakota Democrat was really an evangelical, despite the fact that he had studied for the Methodist ministry at Garrett Theological Seminary. But they had no reason to challenge the evangelical credentials of McGovern's Republican colleague, Mark O. Hatfield of Oregon, a Baptist and cosponsor of the McGovern-Hatfield Amendment to End the War in Vietnam. Hatfield unequivocally identified himself with the tradition of progressive evangelicalism, including education, orphanages, "social outreach to the other less fortunate people," as well as the strong suspicion of militarism that motivated the McGovern-Hatfield Amendment. "That's the rich heritage of the evangelical church," Hatfield said.[54]

Harold E. Hughes rose from being a truck driver to three-term governor of Iowa to become Hatfield's colleague in the U.S. Senate. Hughes was a recovering alcoholic and a lay Methodist preacher. A progressive evangelical, Hughes eliminated capital punishment in the state, increased support for public education, and addressed the problems of poverty as governor, explicitly calibrating his policies to the words of Jesus: "As you did it to one of the least of these my brethren you did it to me." Hughes, a veteran of World War II, questioned the morality of the war in Vietnam and even questioned whether, especially in an age of such destructive weapons technology, any modern war could be considered a "just war."[55]

This roll call of progressive evangelicalism is suggestive and by no means exhaustive. Like all mortals, each of these progressive evangelicals was a product of time and place, each of them bound, to a greater or lesser degree, by the prejudices of the day. It's easy, for example, especially in hindsight, to criticize evangelical racial attitudes in the nineteenth century for being more paternalistic than egalitarian or to criticize McPherson for becoming a tad too exercised over Darwinism. All of these evangelicals took biblical teachings seriously, but what set them apart was their willingness to transcend narrow, pinched interpretations in favor of a broader, more capacious understanding of the mandates of the gospel. The Bible, after all, admits of many interpretations. As Jimmy Carter noted about his fellow Southern Baptists, the leaders of his denomination have the option of cherry-picking verses from the Bible to justify restrictions on women's ministry, or they could take the larger view, which would countenance such evidence as how Jesus himself treated women or St. Paul's declaration that in Christ there is no distinction between slave or free, male or female. He might have added that the former, literalistic approach to the Bible was not all that different from the one employed for centuries to justify slavery.[56]

Progressive evangelicalism generally has aspired to the broader view, and in so doing, the tradition has challenged not only those with more cramped readings of the Bible but also, in many cases, the prevailing social norms. When Charles Finney welcomed women to testify publicly in religious gatherings, for example, he was defying the social conventions of his day. When he and other evangelicals condemned the excesses of capitalism, advocating a moral economy rather than a market economy, they set themselves against the regnant economic thinking of the nineteenth century. The evangelical advocates for peace or common schools or prison reform or labor rights had little to gain personally from their causes, and their advocacy very often aligned them against powerful interests; but they persevered because they believed they were obeying the mandates of the gospel and the command of Jesus to care for "the least of these."

5

THY KINGDOM COME
The Argot of Apocalypticism in American Culture

On the evening of Good Friday, 1878, Charles Taze Russell and a handful of followers, all clad in white robes, gathered at the Sixth Street Bridge in Pittsburgh to await the Millennial Dawn, their translation into heaven. His study of the Scriptures had convinced Russell, a haberdasher from Allegheny, Pennsylvania, that Christ had returned invisibly in 1874 and that now, three and a half years later, the kingdom of God would begin and the faithful would be summoned to heaven. Russell later denied the incident—Pittsburgh newspapers insisted otherwise—and he revised his theology to accommodate this disappointment. The kingdom of Jehovah, he said, would begin in 1914, whereupon God and Satan would rule the world jointly until the battle of Armageddon vanquished the forces of evil and inaugurated a theocratic millennium.[1]

Almost half a century earlier, another self-educated student of the Bible named William Miller, formerly a farmer in Low Hampton, New York, calculated the date of Christ's return on the basis of the apocalyptic writings in the Bible, particularly the New Testament book of Revelation and the prophecies of Daniel in the Hebrew Bible (the Christian Old Testament). The 2,300 days until the cleansing of the temple, spoken of in Daniel 8:14, Miller insisted, should actually be taken as 2300 years, beginning with the decree of Artaxerxes in 457 B.C.E. to rebuild Jerusalem. Simple arithmetic led him to pinpoint the year 1843 as the time of Christ's advent. In 1831 Miller began touring the Northeast with news of his discovery.

By Miller's own reckoning, he preached about 4500 lectures to half a million people between 1831 and 1844. Second Advent associations sprouted up in small towns all over the Northeast. In March 1840 the movement began publishing *Signs of the Times*, a monthly newspaper that eventually became a weekly. The organization also added a daily newspaper, *Midnight Cry*, a penny paper called the *Trumpet of Alarm*, another weekly called *Second Advent Harbinger*, and the *Voice of Elijah*, published by sympathizers in Montreal. A woman in Boston, Clarinda S. Minor, presided as editor of the *Advent Message to the Daughters of Zion*. Out west, the *Western Midnight Cry* emanated briefly from Cincinnati and *Glad Tidings of the Kingdom to Come* from Rochester. In 1842 Millerites published their own hymnal, *Millennial Harp and Millennial Musings*.[2]

William Miller's followers did not rely on literature alone to disseminate their message. Prophetic charts proliferated, detailing Miller's calculations, illustrated with time lines, church ages, and the various beasts of Daniel and Revelation. Armed with these three-by-six-foot banners, itinerant lecturers fanned out across the new nation to apprize audiences of the impending conclusion of human history and inform them of their peril unless they repented. Miller even took a page from the Methodists, the acknowledged masters at popular communication in the nineteenth century, and purchased what was reputedly the largest tent in America (120 yards in circumference with a 55-foot center pole).[3]

As 1843 approached, anticipation and enthusiasm among Miller's fifty thousand followers reached a fever pitch. Preparations for the apocalypse had grown so pervasive that Horace Greeley published an "extra" edition of the *New-York Tribune* on March 2, 1843, to refute William Miller's calculations. Pressed by his followers for a more precise date, Miller declared that the advent would occur sometime between March 21, 1843, and March 21, 1844, which Miller claimed was the Jewish year 5602. By May 2, 1844, Miller acknowledged his error but urged his followers to remain vigilant. An associate later convinced him that he had failed to account for a "tarrying time," so Miller returned to his calculations and emerged with a new date for Christ's return: October 22, 1844.

Preparations resumed. While their crops remained unharvested and their stores shuttered, Millerites gave away their possessions and settled their accounts, both spiritual and temporal. Banks, financial agencies, even the U.S. Treasury, according to contemporary newspaper accounts, recorded large influxes of money to satisfy outstanding obligations. As October 22 dawned, Millerites gathered in their societies to await their elevation to glory; according to some accounts (hotly denied by Adventists), Millerites dressed in white muslin "ascension robes" and waited in cemeteries. But on October 23 they returned home, bitter and disappointed, and succumbed to the mockery of their neighbors. William Miller himself died lonely and forgotten in 1849, but the movement he inspired eventually regrouped after the Great Disappointment of 1844 and became known as the Seventh-day Adventists. Today, Miller's theological descendants claim a worldwide following well in excess of eighteen million.[4]

Americans have long evinced a fascination with the end of time and the role that they would play in such an apocalypse. Even Christopher Columbus invested the discovery of the New World with millennial significance. "God made me the messenger of the new heaven and the new earth of which he spoke in the Apocalypse of St. John after having spoke of it through the mouth of Isaiah," Columbus wrote in 1500, "and he showed me the spot where to find it."[5]

More often, millennial ideas have issued in the expectation that human history might screech to a halt at any moment and dissolve into some kind of apocalyptic judgment. These chiliastic notions, grounded in a literalistic interpretation of biblical prophecies, admit of many different constructions, and evangelicals who agree on such issues as biblical inerrancy (that divine inspiration rendered the Scriptures without error in the original autographs) and church polity will argue bitterly over whether or not God's elect will go through the tribulation—seven years of rule by the antichrist—predicted in Revelation. Will the rapture—Christ's return to summon the faithful, predicted in 1 Thessalonians 4—occur before, during, or after the tribulation? Who is the whore of Babylon described in Revelation 17? American Protestants have generally settled on the Roman Catholic Church as the only logical choice, but they disagree more often on the identity of the antichrist. Napoleon? The pope? Adolph Hitler? John Kennedy? Henry Kissinger? Some speculation even centered around Ronald Wilson Reagan (because he has six letters in each of his three names, corresponding to the mark of the beast, 666, foretold in Revelation 13:18), Mikhail Gorbachev (the birthmark on his forehead), or even Bill Gates—a rumor circulated, appropriately, on the internet (apparently, by some reckonings, if you assign ASCII numbers to the letters of his given name, they total 666).[6]

Will the millennium, one thousand years of godly rule on earth, take place before or after the rapture? The possibilities admit of many combinations: pretrib postmillennialists, midtrib premillennialists, posttrib postmillennialists, pretrib premillennialists, and so on. For at least three centuries now, columns of the faithful have mustered to wage these theological battles and to propagate what is certainly, they contend, the only possible construction of these recondite passages.[7]

Throughout American history, evangelicals have vacillated between pre- and postmillennialism. While the Puritans were decidedly premillennial in their views—that is, they knew that Christ's return could take place at any moment—the revivals of the Great Awakening of the 1730s and 1740s promoted a sense that God was even now working on earth to establish his millennial kingdom. No less a figure than Jonathan Edwards, regarded by many as one of America's premier intellects, believed that the millennium would begin in America. The Society of Believers in Christ's Second Appearing, better known as the Shakers, held that Christ had returned in the person of Mother Ann Lee and that they were busy establishing the millennial kingdom. "The gospel of Christ's Second Appearing," according to the Shakers' Millennial Laws, "strictly forbids all private union between the two sexes, in any case, place, or under any circumstances, in doors or out." John Humphrey Noyes, founder of the Oneida Community in western New York, also believed that Christ had returned (in 70 C.E.), but for him the millennium provided sexual license in the form of "complex marriage."[8]

Various historical events of the eighteenth and nineteenth centuries stirred apocalyptic sentiments and raised postmillennial aspirations. Many of the Patriots in the eighteenth century fused millennial expectations with radical Whig ideology and greeted the American Revolution as "the sacred cause of liberty." While wandering through western Pennsylvania in 1779, Hermon Husband, a New Light evangelical, former North Carolina Regulator, and ardent antifederalist, came upon the eastern corner of the New Jerusalem. "I saw therein the Sea of Glass, the Situation of the Throne; which Sea was as clear as crystal Glass," Husband recalled. "I also saw the Trees of Life, yielding their monthly Fruit; and the Leaves of the Trees healing the Nations; one of which leaves I got hold of, and felt its healing Virtue to remove the Curse and Calamities of Mankind in this World."[9]

Amid the Second Great Awakening, with all of America intoxicated with Arminian self-determinism, an air of optimism about the perfectibility both of humanity and society prevailed; postmillennialism, the doctrine of Christ's triumphal reign on earth, suited the mood, and it complemented nicely the Enlightenment's sanguine appraisal of human potential. This spirit of optimism unleashed all manner of reform efforts—temperance, abolitionism, prison and educational reform, missions—consonant with the assurance that Christ was even then vanquishing the powers of evil and establishing his kingdom.[10]

Julia Ward Howe's "Battle Hymn of the Republic" popularized this triumphalism—the kingdom of God as a juggernaut—during the Civil War.

Mine eyes have seen the glory
of the coming of the Lord:
He is trampling out the vintage
where the grapes of wrath are stored;
He hath loosed the fateful lightning
of his terrible swift sword:
His truth is marching on.[11]

In only slightly more prosaic terms, the Reverend William Gaylord of Fitzwilliam, New Hampshire, echoed this sentiment. "Oh! what a day will that be for our beloved land, when carried through a baptism of fire and blood, struggling through a birth-night of terror and darkness, it shall experience a resurrection to a new life, and to a future whose coming glory already gilds the mountain tops," the Congregationalist minister said. "The day of the Lord is at hand!"[12]

Yet even in the heady days of evangelical reform and utopian idealism in the first half of the nineteenth century, postmillennialism could not claim a monopoly on evangelical eschatology. Sobered by the excesses of the French Revolution, many evangelicals had tempered their optimism about the perfectibility of humanity and society and reverted to premillennialism. William Miller's adventist sentiments were unmistakably premillennial. Joseph Smith's apocalyptic notions led him in a slightly different direction. Convinced that the New Jerusalem would center in Jackson County, Missouri, Smith led a surveying party there, and on May 19, 1838, he staked out the holy city of Adam-ondi-Ahman. Persecution from neighbors and Smith's assassination in 1844 interrupted the preparations for the coming kingdom, but in recent years a small band of Mormons has returned to resume the task, to await the resurrection of Adam, the prophets, and church leaders, and the onset of the millennium.[13]

Among antebellum blacks, mired in slavery, apocalypticism took yet another form, a conviction that God sanctioned rebellion against white slaveholders, whose oppressions marked them for divine judgment. On May 12, 1828, according to Nat Turner, God appeared to the slave preacher in Southampton County, Virginia, and, "I heard a loud noise in the heavens, and the Spirit instantly appeared to me and said the Serpent was loosened, and Christ had laid down the yoke he had borne for the sins of men, and that I should take it on and fight against the Serpent, for the time was fast approaching when the first should be last and the last should be first." Thus emboldened, Nat Turner unleashed his apocalypse on August 21, 1831, a rebellion that claimed the lives of fifty-five whites and two hundred blacks. David Walker, a free black, tried to sear the conscience of slaveholders with predictions of impending judgment: "O Americans! Americans!! I call God—I call angels—I call men, to witness, that your *DESTRUCTION is at hand*, and will be speedily consummated unless you *REPENT*."[14]

With some important exceptions, postmillennialism generally prevailed among American evangelicals until the latter half of the nineteenth century. In the decades following the Civil War, however, much of the optimism about society's perfectibility began to dissipate. As the nation urbanized and industrialized, as waves of European immigrants, most of them Catholic, reached American shores, evangelicals lost their hegemony. Teeming, squalid cities and rapacious industrialists hardly looked like fixtures of a millennial kingdom. Society was not improving, becoming more Christian; it was degenerating, falling into enemy hands. America, moreover, began importing alien notions: Charles Darwin's theory of natural selection, which, pressed to its logical conclusions, undermined literal understandings of Scripture; and the German discipline of textual criticism, or higher criticism, which attacked the integrity of the Bible itself.[15]

In the face of such degeneration, evangelicals began to revise their eschatology. Postmillennialism, with its optimism about the perfectibility of culture before the apocalypse, no longer fit, so American evangelicals cast about for an alternative, which they found in John Nelson Darby's dispensational premillennialism. Darby, a member of the Plymouth Brethren in England, believed that all of history could be divided into seven dispensations and that the present age, "the age of the church," immediately preceded the rapture of the church, the seven-year tribulation, and the coming kingdom of God.[16]

Darby's novel ideas, grounded in typology, numerology, and literalistic interpretations of the Bible, perfectly suited the temper of evangelicals in the late nineteenth century. Instead of a society on a steady course of amelioration, they saw a society careening toward judgment. Increasingly pushed to the margins of American culture, evangelicals—many of whom became fundamentalists after the turn of the century—began to espouse a theology that looked toward the imminent return of Christ to claim his followers and prosecute his judgment against a sinful nation.

More often than not, this conviction prompted evangelicals to separate themselves from the corruption they saw everywhere around them. "I don't find any place where God says the world is to grow better and better, and that Christ is to have a spiritual reign on earth of a thousand years," the popular evangelist Dwight L. Moody declared confidently in 1877. "I find that the earth is to grow worse and worse, and that at length there is going to be a separation." At the turn of the century, John Alexander Dowie, a pentecostal faith healer, attracted 7500 followers to live in his utopian community, Zion City, Illinois, which he believed was the New Zion predicted in the book of Revelation and whose official incorporation in 1902 marked the beginning of the millennial drama. In some cases, especially early in the twentieth century, the rhetoric of evangelicals betrayed a thinly veiled contempt for the culture that had spurned them. "It is a great thing to know that everything is going on according to God's schedule," William Pettingill told an audience of premillennialists in 1919. "We are not surprised at the present collapse of civilization; the Word of God told us all about it."[17]

As American culture and modernity itself turned increasingly hostile in the early decades of the twentieth century, evangelicals continued their turn inward. Reeling from the ignominy of the Scopes Trial in 1925, they immersed themselves in dispensational ideology, with its implicit condemnation of American culture. The *Scofield Reference Bible*, compiled by Cyrus Ingerson Scofield, provided a dispensational template through which evangelicals read the Scriptures. This Bible, first published by Oxford University Press in 1909, became enormously popular among evangelicals and fundamentalists and remains a strong seller, even though supplanted in some ways by an updated version, the *Ryrie Study Bible*, published in 1978.[18]

Premillennial sentiments and apocalyptic prophecies continue to inform evangelical views of the world. Sometimes they have political implications, such as the unconditional evangelical support for Israel, which, evangelicals believe, enjoys God's blessing and will play a critical role in the apocalypse. Or consider the remark made before the House interior committee by James Watt, U.S. secretary of the interior from 1981 to 1983. "I do not know how many future generations we can count on before the Lord returns," he said, an apparent refutation to arguments for conserving natural resources. In the 1990s a number of evangelical groups cooperated with Jews in the task of breeding red heifers in anticipation of the rebuilding of the temple in Jerusalem and the restoration of animal sacrifices there.[19]

But more often apocalyptic convictions form the core of personal piety. Absorbed in the prophetic writings of the Bible, evangelical and fundamentalist preachers regularly exhort their congregations to prepare for the end, to repent and bring their neighbors to Christ. For most, it is not a matter of *if* Christ will return, but *when*. This "blessed hope" provides strength and succor while setting the believers apart from a world that awaits judgment. The words of an evangelical hymn, "This world is not my home, I'm just a-passing through," express both a discomfiture with the dominant culture and an expectation of a superior reward in the hereafter.[20]

How pervasive are these sentiments in American culture? Several indices, admittedly impressionistic and anecdotal, hint at the popularity of these ideas. In the late sixties and early seventies, Herbert W. Armstrong convinced many of his followers to surrender their assets to his Worldwide Church of God in anticipation of Christ's return in 1972. First published in 1970, *The Late Great Planet*

Earth, which posits the imminent collapse of the world in apocalyptic judgment, has sold over fifteen million copies. The *New York Times* named its author, Hal Lindsey, the best-selling author of the 1970s, and the book also inspired a movie by the same title, released in 1977 and narrated by Orson Welles. Billy Graham, the renowned evangelist, shared similar premillennial views, a preoccupation suggested by the titles of two books: *Till Armageddon* and *Approaching Hoofbeats: The Four Horsemen of the Apocalypse.*[21]

These examples only hint at the popular hold of millennial notions in American culture; surely the fifteen million buyers of *The Late Great Planet Earth* included a generous sprinkling of the curious among the faithful. Yet for many in the evangelical subculture, apocalyptic imagery functions as a kind of vernacular, a common language of discourse. The books of Daniel and Revelation provide a lodestar to navigate an increasingly perilous world.

Aside from their convictions about the literal truth of the Bible, evangelicals have many reasons for their fixation with the end of time. First, although this may seem improbable to those outside the evangelical subculture, it's a lot of fun. Evangelicals enjoy speculating about prophetic events. Just who *is* the antichrist? Could those UPC codes in the supermarket someday be imbedded on the back of your hand for use as a kind of debit card, thereby comprising the dreaded and pernicious mark of the beast? How do Desert Storm and the Persian Gulf War or the emergence of the Islamic State fit into the prophetic scheme? Should true believers oppose the United Nations and the European Community as harbingers of the one-world government that would facilitate the rise of the antichrist? Some evangelicals thought the Orwellian year 1984 would herald the end of human history; later, similar predictions shifted to the year 2000. While it is true that such speculations too often lead to paranoia and conspiracy theories, most discussions of this sort are rather innocuous.

Second, a preoccupation with the end times allows for flights of fancy about the shape of a new and perfect world, a chance to start over. These visions about a new heaven and new earth have had a deleterious effect on evangelical engagements in this world; pre-millennialism served to absolve them from responsibility for social amelioration. Ever since the late nineteenth century and at least until the emergence of the Religious Right in the late 1970s, far too many evangelicals have retreated into a bunker mentality, reminding themselves that this world is getting worse, that the only hope is the imminent return of Jesus, and mollifying themselves with blueprints of the heavenly city.

A fixation on the prophecies in the Bible, moreover, places evangelicals in control of history. It allows them to assert that they alone understand the mind of God; they alone have unlocked the mysteries of the Scriptures. The corollary to this smugness, of course, is that everyone else is still benighted; they are lost in darkness—and they await divine judgment—because they have refused to take the apocalyptic prophecies seriously.

Finally, and most importantly, evangelicals see the end times as a summons to conversion, and many pray fervently for a Third Great Awakening. We must set our lives and our hearts in order before Jesus returns, they insist, before it's too late. Is *my* heart right with God? What about family and loved ones? For evangelicals, the prospect of apocalypse is ultimately a call to repentance.

6

A PENTECOST OF POLITICS

Evangelicals and Public Discourse

I could make my point by inviting you to accompany me on a field trip. Our first stop would be the redoubtable Gothic structure of St. Patrick's Cathedral on Fifth Avenue in New York City. There, at high mass on Sunday morning, as the cardinal stepped up to the pulpit, you might well be impressed by the sight of a real-life cardinal—in living color, as the folks at NBC, just across the street in Rockefeller Center, used to say. Before long, however, your thoughts and your mind would wander. Your eyes would probably settle on the tourists walking past, who themselves had taken only momentary notice of the bespectacled older man in the funny costume, reading from a prepared text. And if I asked you twenty minutes after the service to recount for me the highlights of the cardinal's homily, I suspect that you would return the vacant stare of some hapless undergraduate who has just been asked to identify *dispensational premillennialism* on a midterm examination.

Our second stop would be the True Bibleway Church of the Lord Jesus Christ of the Apostolic Faith in Natchez, Mississippi. The Sunday morning service has been going for two hours before Andre Ramsey steps to the pulpit. Pastor Elder Ramsey, as he is known to his congregation, is a self-educated man who supports himself as a lineman for the local utility company. He draws no salary whatsoever for serving as pastor of three churches in Mississippi, each of which he has built from scratch. You won't understand every word of Pastor Elder Ramsey's sermon, but you won't forget it either. And somewhere amid the jumping, the gesticulation, the frenzy, the pauses, and the ululation, you recognize that this man may not be able to rehearse the teleological argument for the existence of God, but he knows how to communicate.

These are, admittedly, two extreme examples, but they illustrate the extent to which evangelicals understand the importance of communication. They have mastered the fine art of oral discourse, especially persuasive rhetoric, in a nation of talkers. I can think of no other culture so enamored of the human voice. We have talk radio and talk television, CB radios and cellular telephones. Letters, more often than not, are bills or legal documents or solicitations, not personal communications; we do that over the telephone.

The oral culture in America derives at least in part from Americans' disdain for tradition. In the religious arena, Americans have always looked askance at creeds, formality, and liturgical rubrics. Indeed, the centrality of discourse in American evangelicalism is a direct legacy of the Protestant Reformation. Martin Luther understood the power of the spoken word to educate, to communicate, to mobilize. The extent to which evangelicals have appropriated that lesson is reflected both in their architecture and in their orders of worship. In high-church traditions, the altar is central, and the entire liturgy leads up to the Eucharist. In most evangelical churches, on the other hand, the pulpit is center stage, and the service reaches its crescendo in the sermon, the spoken word.

Throughout American history, evangelical preachers have also regarded the sermon as a performance, a species of entertainment. George Whitefield, trained in the London theater, understood that no less than Lorenzo Dow, Billy Sunday, Jimmy Swaggart, T. D. Jakes, or Joel Osteen.

Evangelicalism's skill at popular communication—and the use of communications technology—belies its image as somehow backward or retrograde. Even a cursory review of American history suggests more than a casual connection between religious and political communications. As Harry Stout has shown, the persuasive rhetoric of evangelists during the Great Awakening provided a model for Patriot agitators during the Revolutionary era. The communications networks that evangelicals established helped to knit together thirteen disparate colonies. The Methodist circuit riders of the early nineteenth century brought evangelical religion to the frontier, and their organizational genius almost certainly provided the model for grassroots political organizations. As Alexis de Tocqueville observed in 1835, the "two chief weapons which parties use in order to obtain success are the *newspapers* and *public associations*." No one understood both better than antebellum evangelicals, with their presses, their denominations, and their benevolent societies. The political devices of torchlight parades, tents, and urgent calls for commitment, according to Daniel Walker Howe, were taken directly from revival preachers. National political conventions, whose purpose was to galvanize support and whip up enthusiasm, were copied from social reform organizations populated overwhelmingly by evangelicals.[1]

In the burgeoning cities of the latter half of the nineteenth century, political rallies mimicked the great urban crusades of Dwight Lyman Moody, J. Wilbur Chapman, and Billy Sunday, including their use of publicity, advertising, and prodigious advance work. In the early twentieth century, preachers like Aimee Semple McPherson were communicating their evangelical gospel over the radio airwaves in the decade before Franklin Roosevelt discovered the radio as a political tool. So too the televangelists of the 1970s used the emerging technology of satellites and the deregulation of the airwaves to communicate their gospel on television well in advance of Ronald Reagan's masterful use of the medium for his own political ends.

Many politicians throughout American history have appropriated the language, the style, and the fervor of the preacher. Abraham Lincoln adopted the magisterial cadences of the King James Version.

Various preacher-politicians have risen to great heights of oratorical passion. Patrick Henry, who was influenced by the Presbyterian itinerant Samuel Davies, introduced evangelistic fervor, complete with histrionics and rhetorical flourishes, into the world of Virginia politics. The famous "Cross of Gold" speech by William Jennings Bryan, the "Great Commoner," was replete with religious imagery. Bryan's oratory electrified the Democratic National Convention in 1896, and perhaps it is no coincidence that when Bryan himself recalled that famous speech, he remembered that in between the interruptions of tumultuous cheering, "the room was as still as a church." In some cases, especially among African Americans, the line between preacher and politician has been exceedingly vague, even nonexistent. Throughout American history black preachers have served as oracles for their people on both religious and political matters. You need not like his politics to appreciate Jesse Jackson's oratorical artistry before the Democratic conventions of 1984 and 1988. Even though Jackson was not at the top of his form at the latter event in Atlanta, his performance provided a sharp contrast to the careful, measured delivery of his party's presidential nominee, Michael Dukakis. Barack Obama's oratory, inspired in part by black preachers, fueled his meteoric rise to the presidency.[2]

The parallels between evangelical discourse and political rhetoric, however, reach well beyond style. Relentless evangelical harangues directed against the settled clergy in the eighteenth century prefigured the Revolutionary assaults on deference, privilege, and taxation without representation. In the early republic, the massive conversion of American Protestants from Calvinism to Arminianism was no accident. Arminian theology, with its emphasis on the ability of individuals to control their religious destinies, held considerable appeal to a people who had only recently taken their political destiny into their own hands. Those Calvinists who tried to block this democratization of theology were held up to ridicule. Peter Cartwright, for example, a Methodist revivalist during the Second Great Awakening, criticized "some of the old starched Presbyterian preachers" who opposed the revival. In short, evangelical theology had to adjust to a people intoxicated with self-determinism, and the rhetoric of choice, individualism, and optimism pervaded both political and religious discourse throughout most of the antebellum period. It is no coincidence, moreover, that the language of millennialism early in the nineteenth century tended more often than not to assign the United States a special place in the divine economy.[3]

Evangelical rhetoric in the decades following the Civil War was less edifying, but it reflected, once again, the sentiments of many Americans who felt displaced and threatened by rapid urbanization, the incursion of non-Protestant immigrants (most of whom did not share evangelical scruples about temperance), and the corruption of big-city politics. In 1892, for instance, Charles H. Parkhurst, pastor of the Madison Square Presbyterian Church in New York City, unleashed a blistering attack against the Tammany Hall political machine and the police department, which he characterized as "a lying, perjured, rum-soaked and libidinous lot" who were "filthifying our entire municipal life, making New York a very hotbed of knavery, debauchery and bestiality."[4]

Evangelical rhetoric in the twentieth century was marked by dualism—us versus them, the righteous versus the unrighteous, America versus the world. Although evangelicals by and large had retreated from the public arena in the middle half of the twentieth century (from 1925 to 1975), their dualistic perspectives nevertheless fit quite comfortably with a nation mired in two world wars, a "police action," and Indochina. Recall, for instance, Billy Sunday's "hang the kaiser" rallies and persistent evangelical denunciations of "godless communism," which reached their apotheosis during the McCarthy era.

All of this suggests a correlation between evangelical rhetoric and public discourse. Throughout American history the relentless populism that has animated evangelicalism has both reflected and influenced political and cultural currents. Evangelical religion and American politics are so interconnected that it is extraordinarily difficult to determine causation. In religious terms, this symbiosis has been a mixed blessing. At its best it has checked clerical arrogance and ensured at least a measure of accountability. At its worst it has given rise to "wind-sock theology," an evangelicalism that spins constantly in response to the gusts of culture. The shift from Calvinist to Arminian theology in the early republic provides one such example. A better example occurred in the 1980s with the rise of prosperity theology during the Reagan years. The coincidence was, in fact, no coincidence at all. The decade marked by excess, self-aggrandizement, sybaritic leisure, and the headlong quest for affluence found a theological legitimation of sorts in the tortured exegesis of the televangelists who promised jewelry, furs, vacation homes, and fancy automobiles to the faithful—all in the name of Jesus. This was evangelicalism's version of "trickle-down" economics. Prosperity in this case would trickle down from heaven, but it would reach the faithful, of course, only after it had cycled through the rain barrel of the televangelists themselves.

The correlation between Reaganism and the prosperity gospel underscores yet another parallel between evangelicalism and the public arena—namely, the relative absence of ideological ballast. Populist evangelical theology in America, like populist politics, operates on pragmatism more often than principle. Put simply, neither can afford the luxury of ideological baggage. At an early stage in Billy Graham's career, he turned aside a friend's challenge to attend Princeton Theological Seminary and become conversant with intellectual and theological issues. "I don't have the time, the inclination, or the set of mind to pursue them," Graham protested. "I have found that if I say, 'The Bible says' and 'God says,' I get results. I have decided I am not going to wrestle with these questions any longer." When writing about American religion in 1855, Philip Schaff noted that Americans were active rather than contemplative, "more like the busy Martha than like the pensive Mary." American religion, he said, cannot claim "the substratum of a profound and spiritual theology." Neither can American politics claim any secure ideological foundation.[5]

Evangelicals, then, have shaped public discourse both in style and content, and vice versa. In so doing, evangelicalism alternately reflects and determines cultural trends. But if evangelicals generally have a knack for discerning the pulse of American popular sentiment, no figure in American history has refined that sense better than the itinerant preacher, who has served as a kind of bellwether through successive stages of American history.

In the eighteenth century, the evangelical itinerant represented a threat to the established order. Puritanism in New England had collapsed beneath its own weight, but it left behind a state-supported, settled clergy that was increasingly jealous of its prerogatives. A similar situation obtained in the Middle Colonies and the Chesapeake, where the clergy hid behind the redoubt of either orthodoxy or ecclesiology or some combination of the two.

Itinerant preachers flushed them out and, in the process, helped to reshape American culture. They unleashed a wholesale assault on clerical pretensions and complacency. Many of the clergy in the Middle Colonies had become ministers and had migrated to the New World in order to advance their social standing. What they faced instead was the obloquy of itinerants animated by evangelical Pietism. In the Raritan Valley, Theodorus Jacobus Frelinghuysen sounded a distinctly populist theme when he railed against the well-connected, orthodox clergy in New York. Frelinghuysen suggested that "it has been very true that the largest portion of the faithful have been poor and of little account in the world." Gilbert Tennent's famous sermon, *The Danger of an Unconverted Ministry*, delivered at Nottingham, Pennsylvania, on March 8, 1740, and published later the same year, lamented the sinful condition of the colonial clergy and urged the faithful to seek their spiritual sustenance elsewhere. Similarly, John Henry Goetschius delivered himself of the view that "most of the ministers in this country were unregenerate ministers" and some "had already preached many people into hell." When called to account for his charges, Goetschius refused to acknowledge that ecclesiastical authorities had any jurisdiction over him and declared that those who opposed his peregrinations "were plainly godless people."[6]

The situation in New England was hardly more congenial to the enemies of evangelicalism. Itinerants like James Davenport, Timothy Allen, Benjamin Pomeroy, Eleazar Wheelock, Samuel Buell, and Andrew Croswell, among many others, directly challenged both the settled clergy and the standing order. "In Times past there hath been *Order* in the Churches of Christ, *instead of Religion*," Croswell wrote in 1742. "The Truth is, God never works *powerfully*, but Men cry out of *Disorder*: for God's *Order* differs vastly from their *nice* and *delicate* Apprehensions of it." The more radical itinerants became the sworn enemies of order and decorum, and their assault culminated in the bonfires of the Shepherd's Tent, a New Light seminary in New London, Connecticut.[7]

How did the colonial itinerants shape public discourse in the eighteenth century? In form, of course, they introduced extemporaneous preaching. The preeminent practitioner was George Whitefield, the "Grand Itinerant," who skillfully mixed evangelical rhetoric with dramatic devices that left his audiences awestruck. Whitefield's gift for oratorical persuasion is well documented by everyone from Nathan Cole, a Connecticut farmer, to Benjamin Franklin, no friend of organized religion, who, upon hearing Whitefield on Society Hill in Philadelphia, emptied his pockets to support Whitefield's orphanage in Georgia, despite his expressed skepticism about the wisdom of the enterprise. Whitefield and the eighteenth-century itinerants altered forever the character of religious discourse by emphasizing extemporaneous preaching and persuasive rhetoric very much in contrast to the prevailing, more formal modes of address. That oratorical style was critical to the success of the Patriots in the Revolutionary era, and the notion that the vulgar masses needed to be reached directly was a precondition of egalitarianism.

The colonial itinerants reshaped public discourse in still another way—by challenging the established authorities, political and ecclesiastical. New Light Presbyterians and Baptist preachers undermined the gentility of colonial Virginia. The "Associated Pastors of Boston and Charles-Town" did not take kindly to James Davenport's practice of "going with his Friends singing thro' the Streets and High-Ways, to and from the Houses of Worship on Lord's-Days," inviting people to join him for prayer meetings outside of the churches. When Theophilus Pickering accused itinerant Nathaniel Rogers of behavior "subversive of the Order of the Gospel and Peace of the Churches" in 1742, he echoed the sentiments of scores of New England clergy.[8]

The clergy sought and obtained legal recourse against the itinerants, as when Connecticut threatened to banish them from the colony, but the itinerants flouted the laws. The suspicion of clerical pretension reached a fever pitch over the prospect that the Church of England might send a bishop to the American colonies. William Livingston of New York worried publicly about the "ambitious designs" of such a prelate, and the colonists came to regard the Anglican bishop as yet another example of British imperialism and a threat to American liberties. The rhetoric of liberty from ecclesiastical constraints melded almost seamlessly into the language of liberty from political oppression.[9]

The itinerants of the eighteenth century brazenly challenged ecclesiastical hierarchies; their machinations divided churches into revivalist and antirevivalist camps and laid the groundwork for the proliferation of sectarianism in America. Mendicant preachers rent what was left of the unified social fabric in New England by placing revivalist preachers and congregations in competition with the established or "standing order" churches. In time, the evangelical "separates" allied with Enlightenment deists to press for disestablishment in the new nation.

Because of the disestablishment of religion mandated by the First Amendment, the term *dissenter*, applied so liberally to itinerants in eighteenth-century New England, had little resonance in the early republic. Mendicant preachers performed a very different function in the early decades of the nineteenth century. Whereas in the eighteenth century they had *disrupted* the social order, now they *brought* social order to the frontier areas of the new republic. Evangelical itinerants tamed some of the rowdiness of life on the frontier, where lawlessness, alcohol abuse, and violence were rampant.

Once again, however, the message of the itinerants was populist—simple, easy to understand, and delivered extemporaneously. In his autobiography, Richard Allen, founder of the African Methodist Episcopal Church, identified the Methodists as the primary oracles of evangelicalism among African Americans. "We are beholden to the Methodists, under God, for the light of the Gospel we enjoy; for all other denominations preached so high-flown that we were not able to comprehend their doctrine," Allen wrote. "Sure am I that reading sermons will never prove so beneficial to the colored people as spiritual or extempore preaching."[10]

The most spectacular showcase for extemporaneous preaching in the antebellum period was the camp meeting, which attracted both settlers and itinerants from long distances. The evangelical preacher, using the language of the vernacular, attacked and ridiculed Calvinist theology for its elitism. As Nathan Hatch has demonstrated, religion in the early republic—be it Methodism, the Baptists, the Disciples of Christ, the black churches, or Mormonism—was doggedly democratic in spirit and populist in tone, much to the chagrin of the elites. Samuel Goodrich, editor of Boston's first daily newspaper, described "Crazy" Lorenzo Dow as "uncouth in his person and appearance." "It is scarcely possible to conceive of a person more entirely destitute of all natural eloquence," Goodrich wrote. "But he understood common life, and especially vulgar life—its tastes, prejudices and weaknesses; and he possessed a cunning knack of adapting his discourses to such audiences."[11]

The antebellum itinerant brought a measure of order and a distinctly evangelical version of civilization to the frontier, even if it was not the sort of civilization that the eastern elites would endorse. "We had no pewed churches, no choirs, no organs," Peter Cartwright recalled wistfully in 1856. "The Methodists in that early day dressed plain; attended their meetings faithfully, especially preaching, prayer and class meetings; they wore no jewelry, no ruffles."[12]

The itinerant, traveling alone, became a kind of paradigm of American individualism that was embodied also in Jacksonian democracy. He (and sometimes she) harbored a disregard—even disdain—for ecclesiastical hierarchies and authorities as well as for pretension of any sort. The itinerants and their evangelical theology served as a democratic and leveling force. Women exhorted in revival meetings. Female abolitionists appeared before mixed audiences, meaning women and men. Slave preachers addressed white congregations.

As the nineteenth century wore on, convulsed by social, economic, and demographic changes, the evangelical itinerant riding on horseback became the colporteur riding the iron horse. Many circuit riders, such as John Wesley Osborne, made that transition directly. Osborne became a colporteur for the American Tract Society in 1851, and, like the circuit riders in the Jacksonian era, the colporteur system depended upon individualism. The entire scheme, according to the Society, combined "two of the mightiest elements of influence over the human mind . . . *individual christian [sic] example and effort*, and *a sanctified press*."[13]

The society itself traced the practice of distributing Bibles and literature to the Reformation of the sixteenth century and even to the apostles. "Such is *the vastness of the country* as to require, especially in the newer States, an itinerant system of evangelization," the society wrote in 1836. The United States needed schools, colleges, and seminaries, the society declared, "ministers must be multiplied." But the colporteur system offered unique advantages as well as more immediate results. The progress of the gospel in the nineteenth century necessitated "an agency that is truly republican—going as the colporteur does to *all the people*, and first of all to those to whom no one else goes, with means of light and salvation." The society continued its democratic rhetoric: "If we would ignite a mass of anthracite, we must place the kindling at the bottom: if we would kindle the fire of knowledge and piety, we must commence at the lowest point of social being."[14]

Colporteurs not only sold Bibles, but in the course of their peregrinations they also performed marriages, served various missionary functions, set up lending libraries in the "public rooms" of hotels, organized Sunday schools, and preached to various congregations, including those gathered at railroad stations. Once again, evangelical itinerants brought their message to the people. During an era when political campaigns were conducted by rail, Osborne, for instance, traveled over twenty thousand miles in his first year as a colporteur on the Illinois Central Railroad, distributing Bibles, counseling travelers, and forging friendships with porters and conductors.[15]

What was the colporteur's relationship to the larger culture? The Bible peddler took full advantage of the national rise in literacy, but he also functioned as a harbinger of the emerging commercial economy and the culture of consumption. The early literature of the American Tract Society had placed a great deal of emphasis on the need to distribute Bibles—to sell them, if possible, but to give them away if need be. The *Instructions of the Executive Committee of the American Tract Society, to Colporteurs and Agents*, published in 1868, did not disregard altogether the importance of propagating the gospel, but the tone had shifted somewhat. "Though strictly a benevolent enterprise, there are endless details of a business character, requiring as much accuracy and care as in mercantile or banking transactions," the society counseled. The New York office supplied two account books to every colporteur together with detailed instructions about bookkeeping: "As far as possible, fill every blank."[16]

The society also offered advice on sales techniques. "In effecting sales, there will be occasion for all your skill and talent," the *Instructions* stated. "The merchant is unwearied in bringing forward articles to attract the purchaser. . . . Endeavor to secure attention to the contents, character, and usefulness of the books, before asking the family to purchase." The society urged its colporteurs to exhibit their entire line of goods, and it understood the importance of packaging and merchandizing: "Be careful to call attention to the publications for children and youth, which are so beautifully printed and illustrated by engravings so as to tempt every eye, and so rich in spiritual instruction to profit every heart." In the emerging consumer society of the late nineteenth century, the minister had, in effect, become a merchant.[17]

The evangelical itinerants around the turn of the twentieth century, the urban revivalists, also adopted the language of commerce. Billy Sunday, a former baseball player for the Chicago White Stockings, began his evangelistic career barnstorming through the Midwest. After 1912 Sunday took his rallies to the cities, where he promised business and civic leaders that he could revive the churches, end labor unrest, and close the saloons—all for two dollars a head. As Douglas Frank has shown, Sunday, who once declared that he would stand on his head in a mud puddle "if I thought it would help me win souls to Christ," combined personal charisma, colloquial language, and vaudeville antics with an astute business sense. Within a culture that was becoming enamored of statistics, success for Billy Sunday was measured in numbers—attendance at the services, number of converts, total cost of the event. Advertising campaigns, careful planning, and prodigious advance work marked Sunday's campaigns.[18]

Another example of an evangelical itinerant who understood the prevailing mood of the culture was the irrepressible Aimee Semple McPherson. Like thousands of itinerant preachers before her, "Sister Aimee" tirelessly toured the country, and, in an age when the motor car was very much a novelty, she knew how to attract attention. McPherson decorated her "Gospel Auto" with evangelistic slogans and once drove it in a Mardi Gras parade. After she settled in Los Angeles, McPherson's show-business antics rivaled those of Hollywood, across town. Her standard uniform consisted of a white dress, blue cape, and a bouquet of red roses, suggesting that she was playing out her childhood ambition of becoming an actress. On one occasion she rode onto the stage of Angelus Temple astride a motor-cycle, and on another she delivered her sermon, dressed in yellow, from the plaster-of-paris petals of a giant Easter lily.[19]

In 1922 McPherson became the first woman to preach a ser-mon over the radio. Shortly thereafter Angelus Temple estab-lished the first religious radio station, KFSG, thereby heralding yet another—perhaps the final—chapter in the history of evan-gelical itinerancy. Evangelicals' use of the media in the twentieth and twenty-first centuries—both radio and television, and now the internet—has solved forever the problem of itinerancy in American culture because it allows the evangelist, in effect, to be everywhere at once. Evangelicals—from McPherson to Marilyn Hickey, from Charles Fuller and Billy Graham to Jerry Falwell and Frederick Price—have taken full advantage of the latest in com-munications technology. Whereas early in the nineteenth century Methodist circuit riders braved the elements to bring the gospel to the frontier, the radio evangelists of the 1920s and 1930s and the televangelists of the 1970s and 1980s could address the masses from the comfort of a studio.

How has this affected public discourse? Every election year political pundits decry the vacuousness of American political rheto-ric, implying that, in some long-forgotten halcyon age, every matter of public interest was debated fully, intelligently, and without cari-cature. Indeed, there can be little doubt that the electronic media, television especially, have compromised the quality of discourse. The cheapening of discourse, this pandering to the lowest common denominator, applies equally to religion and to politics.

But I wonder if there is anything novel about this. American rhetoric, whether religious or political, has always valued style over substance. After Bryan's stirring speech on the floor of the Demo-cratic convention in 1896, John Peter Altgeld, governor of Illinois, called it "the greatest speech I've ever listened to," but soon there-after asked a friend, "What did he say anyhow?" Millions of auditors throughout American history can attest to the same confusion following an evangelical sermon or a political speech.[20]

The close relationship between evangelical rhetoric and political discourse, however, ensures a continued emphasis on style over substance. The absence of religious hierarchies in American evangelicalism has given rise to the cult of personality. Evangelicals, for the most part, do not organize themselves into churches according to creeds or doctrines or even polity; they galvanize instead around a charismatic leader. Electronic media have only exaggerated this tendency, but it is no less present in politics, especially with the breakdown of grassroots political organizations over the last quarter century. The cult of personality is pervasive both in evangelical religion and in American politics. Popular success in America depends on one's ability to galvanize a following, be it a congregation or a constituency.

In the United States, one of the most reliable ways to do that is to rehearse democratic, populist themes, to rail against pretension and the entrenched elites, whether it be the imperial presidency or the bishop dressed in ecclesiastical finery. The signal contribution of itinerants to American life is the remarkable absence of anticlericalism in the United States. Itinerant preachers ensured this absence with their perorations against clerical arrogance in the eighteenth century, thereby forcing ministers to adopt a popular idiom, both in message and in comportment. Successful politicians have echoed those themes, sometimes disingenuously, to be sure, but effectively nonetheless.

The line between the preacher and the politician in American culture, both in style and in substance, is indeed a thin one. Pastor Elder Ramsey, summoning his congregation to Jesus with his extemporaneous delivery and his religious egalitarianism, has a great deal in common with the stump politician casting for votes. Both understand the value of entertainment, the force of persuasion, and the importance of aligning themselves—rhetorically, at least—against the privileged, the powerful, and the pretentious.

The symbiotic relationship between evangelicalism and public discourse has given both a distinctly populist cast and has led to a melding of styles. Perhaps a woman from Kansas captured this connection best when she described the 1890 political campaign as "a religious revival, a crusade, a pentecost of politics."[21]

7

A LOFTIER POSITION
American Evangelicalism and the Ideal of Femininity

No issue caused evangelicals more consternation in the second half of the twentieth century than feminism. The so-called second wave of American feminism began in 1963 with the publication of *The Feminine Mystique* by Betty Friedan, and the women's movement brought radical changes in gender roles, economic expectations, sexual behavior, the composition of families, and language. In 1945 the number of American women in the labor force stood at 29 percent; by 1970 that number rose to 38 percent, and in 1995 to 46 percent.[1]

The response to the emergence of feminism and the push for equal rights among evangelicals has been both curious and ironic. On the face of it, evangelicals should have embraced feminism—indeed, they should have led the movement—because their forebears in the nineteenth century were in the vanguard of pushing for gender equality and women's suffrage. Some of the most important leaders of nineteenth- and early twentieth-century evangelicalism were women. Instead of adding their voices to the feminist cause, however, many evangelicals in the late twentieth century went through all manner of contortions to oppose it, first by clinging to the nineteenth-century cultural ideal of femininity, with its lionization of female piety as the purest expression of Christianity, and then by lending their support to such organizations as Eagle Forum and Concerned Women for America.

During a 1989 television interview, Bailey Smith, an evangelical and an official in the Southern Baptist Convention, offered his views of women. "The highest form of God's creation," he said, "is womankind." Such pronouncements became so commonplace among American evangelicals late in the twentieth century that it is easy to gloss over their significance. Those who purport to be the guardians of Christian orthodoxy, a tradition that, more often than not, has blamed Eve for Adam's downfall, trumpeted the unique purity of women, the "highest form of God's creation."[2]

These encomiums permeate evangelical piety. If you page through any evangelical songbook published after, say, 1840, you will find all sorts of examples of women alternately praying and weeping for their children, waiting for wayward, sometimes drunken, sons to come home. "Tell Mother I'll be There," for instance, is a forlorn, anguished cry from one such son who wants desperately to assure his mother, now "home with Jesus," that her prayers had been answered. These paeans to female piety intensify as Mother's Day approaches each year.

> Mother is the sweetest word
> You and I have ever heard!
> Mother, oh how dear the thought,
> A bit of heaven you have brought![3]

All of this might be dismissed merely as vulgar sentimentality, the Protestant counterpart to popular Catholic pinings for the Virgin Mary, but the celebration of female piety by evangelicals has a particular focus in the home. If the Blessed Virgin ever sorted socks, scrubbed the kitchen floor, or worried about ring around the collar, we seldom hear about it, even from her most devoted followers.

Not so for evangelical women. Their identity is tied almost exclusively to motherhood and to what one evangelical writer has called "the oft-maligned delights of homemaking." You do not have to look very far in evangelical literature to find celebrations of motherhood and female domesticity. "Raising children is a blessing from the Lord, and I can't imagine a home without the mother being there," Nancy Tucker, a "stay-at-home mother," wrote in an evangelical magazine. "Being a mother, and filling mother's place, is one of the greatest responsibilities there is in this . . . world," an editorial in *The Way of Truth* proclaimed. "Those who feel that a woman is wasting her time, and burying her talents, in being a wife and mother in the home, are simply blinded by the 'gods' of this world." Such domestic duties, the editorial continued, must not be taken lightly. "What a grave and sacred responsibility this is. To provide food, clothing and shelter, may be the easiest part for many couples. To be a true *mother* goes far beyond supplying these temporal needs. The love, the nurturing, the careful guiding, the moral example, the moral teaching, the training, is the most important of all."[4]

An article in *Kindred Spirit*, a magazine published by Dallas Theological Seminary, echoed this theme. "In many ways God measures a woman's success by her relationship with her husband and children," the author, a woman, writes. "Many women ache to learn how to be truly successful in marriage and motherhood."[5]

This ideology, of course, is cloaked in biblical literalism. St. Paul the apostle is not usually remembered as a feminist, and evangelicals generally refuse to see his proscriptions as culturally conditioned. While most evangelicals have maneuvered around Paul's insistence that women keep their heads covered in church, they cannot see—or have elected *not* to see—his commands to keep silent and to be submissive as similarly culture-bound. Consequently, evangelical women are expected to be submissive, to demand no voice of authority in the church or in the home. As the article in *Kindred Spirit* puts it, "Young women need to be taught a biblical view of their roles and relationships with their husbands in order to truly liberate them to be all that God intended them to be and to experience the best that He has for them." Paradoxically, then, evangelical women are supposed to feel a kind of liberation in this submission to their husbands. "In seeking to recognize the crucial role of the husband and father as head of the household," the argument goes, "perhaps we have lost sight of the ways that family warmth is generated by the love and security given by a godly wife and mother."[6]

It was not always so in American history, even in the evangelical tradition. I have already alluded to the discrepancies between historic Christian theology and the contemporary lionization of women by evangelicals. Through the centuries, Christian theology has often regarded women as temptresses, the descendants of Eve, the inheritors of a wicked, seductive sensuality that could only be tempered through subordination to men. John Robinson, pastor of the Pilgrims in Plymouth, Massachusetts, for instance, enjoined a "reverend subjection" of the wife to her husband, adding that she must not "shake off the bond of submission, but must bear patiently the burden, which God hath laid upon the daughters of Eve." The Puritans of New England also imbibed traditional suspicions about women; consider their treatment of Anne Hutchinson, their contempt for the Quakers' egalitarian views of women, and the evident misogyny of the Salem witch hysteria. Cotton Mather, the redoubtable Puritan divine, referred to women as "the hidden ones," a moniker that betrayed his misgivings about female spirituality. More important, the Puritans regarded the man as both head of the household and the person responsible for the spiritual nurture and welfare of his children.[7]

Around the turn of the eighteenth century, however, the sermonic rhetoric in New England signaled a shift in sentiment. Women, who joined the churches in far greater numbers than men, began to be extolled as uniquely tender and loving and, hence, spiritually superior to their husbands, who were increasingly involved in commercial pursuits. Whereas in the Revolutionary era *virtue* was a political term applied to the fusion of civic humanism with evangelical ardor, by the end of the eighteenth century, *virtue* had become synonymous with femininity.

The nineteenth century witnessed a domestic revolution in American life with the romanticization of the home, changes in gender roles, and, finally, the idealization of female piety. While there is some evidence that the republican ideals of the Revolutionary era permeated family life and led, at least for a time, to the relative equality of husbands and wives, the real changes occurred during the Second Great Awakening early in the nineteenth century when women were freed from institutional restraints in the enthusiasm of the revival. The Awakening taught that everyone was equal before God, a notion that combined roughly equal parts of republican ideology and Arminian theology, which emphasized the ability of individuals to initiate the salvation process. Charles Grandison Finney's "new measures," moreover, encouraged women's participation in revival meetings, and evangelical women began to assert themselves as leaders of various benevolent and social reform movements. Some women, such as Phoebe Palmer, Sarah Lankford, and Margaret (Maggie) Van Cott, became influential evangelists.[8]

Despite the temporary loosening of restraints during times of revival, nineteenth-century women rarely ascended to positions of religious authority. Whenever evangelical women aspired to leadership, they were met with stern warnings. Presbyterian minister Ashbel Green, sometime president of the College of New Jersey, reminded his auditors in 1825 that Christ framed women "with that shrinking delicacy of temperament and feeling, which is one of their best distinctions, which renders them amiable." Green acknowledged that such female characteristics, "while it unfits them for command" and "subjects them, in a degree, to the rougher sex, gives them, at the same time, an appropriate and very powerful influence." Green concluded that women could not, however, expect that Christ "who formed them with this natural and retiring modesty, and under a qualified subjection to men, would ever require, or even permit them, to do anything in violation of his own order."[9]

Did this mean that women had no spiritual role to play whatsoever? On the contrary, women must assume responsibility for the home and, in particular, for the spiritual nurture of the children. "The female breast is the natural soil of Christianity," Benjamin Rush, a fervent evangelical, opined. "It is one of the peculiar and most important duties of Christian women," Ashbel Green wrote, "to instruct and pray with children, and to endeavor to form their tender minds to piety, intelligence, and virtue." Here was the proper sphere of female spirituality—as moral guardians of the home, in charge of the religious instruction and nurture of the children. "The family state," Catharine Beecher and Harriet Beecher Stowe wrote in 1869, "is the aptest earthly illustration of the heavenly kingdom, and in it woman is its chief minister."[10]

Nineteenth-century evangelical literature fairly brims with examples of maternal piety and persistent prayers that eventually, sometimes even after her death, effect the conversion of a mother's children. This idea of women as spiritual titans was new in the nineteenth century and peculiar to America. "Although the women of the United States are confined within the narrow circle of domestic life, and their situation is in some respects one of complete dependence," Alexis de Tocqueville, the peripatetic French observer, wrote in 1835, "I have nowhere seen woman occupying a loftier position." After outlining Americans' distinctive and careful division of "the duties of man from those of woman," de Tocqueville attributed America's "singular prosperity and growing strength" to "the superiority of their women." Ann Douglas calls this development the "feminization" of American culture, the product of a collusion between nineteenth-century clergy, whose power and status were waning, and housewives eager for some emotional outlet.[11]

Men came to be characterized as aggressive and indifferent to godliness, whereas women became the lifeblood of the churches. They were the repositories of virtue, meek and submissive—like Jesus himself. Thus, female spirituality was upheld as an ideal, a notion taken to its extremes in Shaker theology and even in Christian Science, both of which asserted explicitly the superiority of the feminine and linked the perfection of humanity to womanhood. Women were implicitly more spiritual in nineteenth-century America. They were morally superior to men; they had a greater capacity for religiosity. Women, therefore, became responsible for the inculcation of virtue into their daughters, sons, and husbands. The evangelical women of Utica, New York, for instance, organized themselves into a Maternal Association that met biweekly and required that each member pledge to pray for her children daily, to read literature on Christian child-rearing, to set a pious example, and to spend the anniversary of each child's birth in fasting and prayer.[12]

Other forces besides revivalism lay behind this transition from the spiritual patriarchy of the Puritan family to the evangelical household of the nineteenth century. The early republic witnessed the gradual emergence of a market economy and the stirrings of nascent industrialization. Men began to work outside the home and the farm. They eventually organized into guilds as their labor became increasingly specialized. Traditional family and kinship networks thus gave way to associations among fellow workers. Families were no longer self-sufficient; they depended on the fathers' wages. Gender roles became more distinct. "From the numerous avocations to which a professional life exposes gentlemen in America from their families," Benjamin Rush wrote, "a principal share of the instruction of children naturally devolves upon the women." Men increasingly distanced themselves from domestic chores and activities, and women succumbed to the "cult of domesticity" or the "cult of true womanhood," marked by purity, piety, and domesticity.[13]

Thus sentimentalized, women assumed responsibility for domestic life, especially the religious instruction of the children. For many, in fact, the two were inseparable. In his *Treatise on Bread, and Bread-Making*, Sylvester Graham, Presbyterian minister, temperance lecturer, and health reformer, explicitly assigned to mothers the responsibility for both the physical and moral well-being of their children. It is the mother, wrote Graham, "who rightly perceives the relations between the dietetic habits and physical and moral condition of her loved ones, and justly appreciates the importance of good bread to their physical and moral welfare." Indeed, the sphere of domesticity—including the home, education and nurture of children, and religious matters generally—was the one area where the nineteenth-century woman reigned supreme, her judgments largely unchallenged. "In matters pertaining to the education of their children, in the selection and support of a clergyman, and in all benevolent enterprises, and in all questions relating to morals or manners, they have a superior influence," Catharine Beecher wrote in *A Treatise on Domestic Economy* in 1841. "In all such concerns, it would be impossible to carry a point, contrary to their judgement and feelings; while an enterprise, sustained by them, will seldom fail of success."[14]

An important theological development—a new focus on religious instruction and socialization—reinforced the importance of female nurture. The tides of revival early in the nineteenth century swept away strict Calvinist doctrines of depravity and original sin, thereby emphasizing the ability of the individual to control his or her spiritual destiny; eventually this downplaying of depravity and the elevation of human volition undermined the traditional emphasis on dramatic conversions. Horace Bushnell's *Christian Nurture*, published in 1847, insisted that children should be reared from birth as though they were Christians, that parents should not expect a dramatic conversion experience in their children. Rather, children should be educated and socialized in such a way that they would always consider themselves Christian or, in Puritan terms, among the elect. Who should perform this duty, especially in a society with increasingly differentiated gender roles? With fathers away at the mill or the factory all day, the task of "Christian nurture" fell to women.

The home thus became the sphere that both defined and, to a degree, delimited female influence. As the Victorian era unfolded, moreover, mechanized production and a commercial economy increasingly eased domestic burdens, especially for the middle-class mother, who very often had a hired girl (usually a recent immigrant) to help with household chores. No longer must a woman spend her hours sewing, weaving, making soap, or butchering meat for her family. Instead, her husband's wages and the commercial economy gave her time to fuss over it. A passel of magazines, such as *Godey's Lady's Book*, instructed the Victorian woman on how to decorate her home with ornate woodworking and carvings and a vast array of furnishings—bookcases, clocks, overstuffed chairs—now within her budget. The invention of the power loom in 1848 made carpets plentiful and affordable. The parlor organ became a kind of domestic shrine, with its high verticality, its carved, pointed arches, and its nooks, crannies, and shelves for family photographs and mementoes. The organ itself, used for family hymn-singing, both symbolized and reinforced religious notions and the ideal of feminine domesticity. *Mother* played the organ and thereby cemented her role as the religious keystone of the family.[15]

These notions about feminine spirituality persisted among evangelicals in the twentieth and twenty-first centuries. Many of the taboos devised by evangelicals in their time of beleaguerment in the 1920s and 1930s centered around women. In reaction to the perceived moral laxity of the larger culture that was careening stubbornly toward judgment, fundamentalists insisted that women forswear worldly adornments, especially jewelry and cosmetics. They devised elaborate parietal rules intended to protect the sexual innocence of their children, especially the girls, who were perceived as vulnerable to the animal cravings of less-spiritual males.

The Victorian myth of feminine spiritual superiority became so entrenched in twentieth-century evangelicalism that many preachers felt obliged to shake men out of their spiritual complacency. Recall, for instance, the machismo posturings of evangelist Billy Sunday, who insisted that in Jesus we find "the definition of manhood." Other evangelists agreed. "God is a masculine God," the firebrand John R. Rice insisted to a male audience in 1947. "God bless women, but He never intended any preacher to be run by a bunch of women." But the intensity of Rice's protestations merely verifies the pervasiveness of the myth. Presbyterian preacher Donald Grey Barnhouse confirmed this in his characterization of a typical Christian household. "The husband is not interested in the things of God, so the family drifts along without any spiritual cohesion," he wrote. "Perhaps they all go to church together on Sunday morning, and the wife goes to all the activities of the week, but the husband seems uninterested." Barnhouse then offered a familiar, albeit paradoxical, prescription for this malaise: feminine submission. "With delight she learns the joy of knowing it is her husband's house, his home; the children are his; she is his wife," he wrote. "When a woman realizes and acknowledges this, the life of the home can be transformed, and the life of her husband also."[16]

This notion reached its apotheosis in the 1970s with the enormous popularity of Marabel Morgan's book *The Total Woman*. The answer to a troubled marriage, Morgan preached, lay in becoming a "Total Woman," a wife who submitted abjectly to her husband and who burrowed herself ever deeper into the putative bliss of domesticity. "A Total Woman caters to her man's special quirks, whether it be in salads, sex, or sports," Morgan wrote. "She makes his home a haven, a place to which he can run."[17]

Against the background of this ideal of feminine domesticity, evangelicals found the rapidly changing views of women in the waning decades of the twentieth century utterly disconcerting. Perhaps nothing—not even Darwinism and higher criticism, the issues of the 1910s and 1920s—so contributed to their sense of cultural dislocation. American evangelicals were caught off guard by *The Feminine Mystique*, and the ensuing feminist movement left them confused and full of resentment, because the domestic ideal that fundamentalism had reified since the nineteenth century was now derided as anachronistic by the broader culture. More confusing still was the fact that many evangelical women, like American women everywhere, had joined the workforce. They were beset on the one hand by calls for liberation and self-assertion from feminists, and they were peppered from the pulpit by insistent rehearsals of the nineteenth-century ideal of femininity. Those who resisted the workplace inevitably felt anger and even shame about being labeled "just a housewife," and they protested loudly, if unconvincingly, about the nobility of tending the home.

Very often, however, general economic stringency, an unemployed husband, or divorce tipped the balance in the general direction of the feminists. But those evangelical women were then left with what Leon Festinger calls cognitive dissonance: the necessity, on the one hand, of employment and, on the other, the compunction they felt about perpetuating evangelical standards. Many felt guilt and confusion for "abandoning" their homes and families, thereby violating the fundamentalist feminine ideal.

A question-and-answer exchange in the May 1989 issue of James Dobson's *Focus on the Family* magazine illustrates poignantly this confusion and anger as well as this pining for a halcyon past. "As a homemaker," the question from an anonymous reader begins, "I resent the fact that my role as a wife and mother is no longer respected as it was in my mother's time. What forces have brought about this change in attitudes in the Western world?" Dobson's response is equally illuminating:

> Female sex-role identity has become a major target for change by those who wish to revolutionize the relationship between men and women. The women's movement and the media have been remarkably successful in altering the way females "see" themselves at home and in society. In the process, every element of the traditional concept of femininity has been discredited and scorned, especially those responsibilities associated with homemaking and motherhood.
>
> Thus, in a short period of time, the term *housewife* has become a pathetic symbol of exploitation, oppression, and—pardon the insult—stupidity, at least as viewed from the perspective of radical feminists. We can make no greater mistake as a nation than to continue this pervasive disrespect shown to women who have devoted their lives to the welfare of their families.

Dobson, of course, failed to acknowledge that his "traditional concept of femininity" (and presumably the one shared by his distraught reader) was a nineteenth-century construct.[18]

More significantly, Dobson's response identified the enemy: "radical feminists," the women's movement, and the media. In the face of such a conspiracy, evangelicals had to muster their troops, something they did with remarkable success in the 1970s and 1980s, but in so doing they were forced to ignore, even to repudiate, the considerable support of evangelicals for women's issues in the nineteenth century. What was especially striking about the exertion of evangelical influence in the American political arena late in the twentieth century was the extent to which issues relating to gender—the Equal Rights Amendment, abortion, private sexual morality—shaped their political agenda. Evangelicals, especially those associated with the Religious Right, regularly attached the sobriquet "antifamily" to policies and to politicians they regarded as inimical, and they have, curiously, attached singular attention to the issue of abortion.

In the ensuing years, evangelicals tried, with considerable success, to propel abortion to the center of political debate. A group of activists calling themselves Operation Rescue picketed and blocked abortion clinics in New York, Atlanta, Wichita, Buffalo, and other cities around the country. Anti-abortion hecklers regularly disrupted Democratic rallies during the 1980s and 1990s.

The Supreme Court's *Roe v. Wade* decision of January 22, 1973, which effectively struck down laws restricting a woman's right to an abortion, was initially greeted with silence or indifference by evangelicals—the Southern Baptist Convention actually endorsed the decision, after having passed an earlier resolution calling for the legalization of abortion—but by the end of the decade, as conservative evangelicals began to mobilize politically, the abortion issue helped to galvanize them into a potent political force. Jerry Falwell, for instance, credited that decision with awakening him from his apolitical stupor, even though he had declared some years earlier that he "would find it impossible to stop preaching the pure saving gospel of Jesus Christ, and begin doing anything else—including fighting Communism, or participating in civil-rights reforms." Falwell thereby articulated a fairly common evangelical attitude in the mid-sixties. "Nowhere are we commissioned to reform the externals," he said. "We are not told to wage war against bootleggers, liquor stores, gamblers, murderers, prostitutes, racketeers, prejudiced persons or institutions, or any other existing evil as such." *Roe v. Wade*, however, together with what Falwell regarded as sundry assaults on the family, triggered an about-face, albeit several years after the decision. By 1979 Falwell had shed his political naïveté and had organized his "Moral Majority" to counter the evil influences in American culture that threatened to subvert the evangelical ideal of femininity.[19]

Abortion violated the cherished evangelical ideal of feminine domesticity. If women guarded their purity and contented themselves with their divinely ordained roles as mothers and housewives, then abortions would be unnecessary. For evangelicals, the very fact that abortion was a political issue in the first place provided an index of how dramatically American culture had deserted their ideal of femininity. The roots of the "disorder," then, could be found in female restiveness, a popular unwillingness to accept the role that God had designed for women. According to Susan Key, a homemaker from Dallas, Texas, who devised a course for women, called Eve Reborn, God gave women "a unique capacity for submission and obedience and when this capacity is thwarted by rebellion and deceit, it becomes a capacity to destroy which begins to work within her heart and then sulks out to her intimate relationships, widens to her acquaintances, to society, and then into history."[20]

But if benighted and wayward women contributed to this massive cultural malaise that evangelicals so decried, women also, because of their exalted spirituality, held the key to redemption. "I firmly believe the role of a woman today is to nurture our next generation," Maxine Sieleman of Concerned Women for America said during the 1988 presidential primaries, thereby echoing nineteenth-century evangelical notions of virtue. "She has the power within her hands to either make or break a nation. A good woman can make a bad man good, but a bad woman can make a good man bad. . . . Women are the real key for turning this country around. . . . I firmly believe that God has always worked through women."[21]

Phyllis Schlafly, who almost singlehandedly defeated the proposed Equal Rights Amendment to the Constitution, said it more succinctly in *The Power of the Positive Woman*. The ideal woman, according to Schlafly, was not merely a housewife but a "patriot and defender of our Judeo-Christian civilization." Moreover, she added, "It is the task of the Positive Woman to keep America good." Compare the sentiments of Catharine Beecher in *A Treatise on Domestic Economy*, published in 1841. "The mother writes the character of the future man; the sister bends the fibres that hereafter are the forest tree; the wife sways the heart, whose energies may turn for good or for evil the destinies of a nation," Beecher wrote. "Let the women of a country be made virtuous and intelligent, and the men will certainly be the same." Beecher added that "the formation of the moral and intellectual character of the young is committed mainly to the female hand."[22]

The agenda of politically conservative evangelicals late in the twentieth century, then, represented an almost desperate attempt to reclaim the nineteenth-century ideal of femininity both for themselves and for a culture that had abandoned that ideal. For American evangelicals, women serve as a kind of bellwether for the culture at large. If women allow themselves to be seduced by the "radical feminists" into abandoning their "God-given" responsibilities in the home, then America is in trouble. If, however, women cling to Victorian notions of submission, nurture, and domesticity, then the future of the republic is secure. Far from the temptress of earlier Christian orthodoxy, the contemporary woman, in the rhetoric of American evangelicalism, can be a redeemer. What better demonstration of her superior spirituality?

Evangelical notions about femininity faced tough opposition late in the twentieth century. Despite their successes in the political arena, American evangelicals remained on the defensive, trying to shore up what the broader culture viewed as a quaint, anachronistic view of women. But the supreme irony is that such contortions were unnecessary, because opposition to feminism ignored the legacy of evangelical activism on behalf of women in the nineteenth century. I've long suspected that the reason for evangelicals' virulent reaction to feminism is that the early leaders of the twentieth-century women's movement were Jewish, which meant that they drew their inspiration from sources other than the New Testament and the ideology of nineteenth-century evangelicalism.

We can only speculate how the political and cultural landscape of the late twentieth century might have been different had evangelicals assumed their rightful place alongside leaders of the feminist movement. Surely the presence of evangelicals would have tempered some of the more radical elements of the women's movement, but it is equally possible that the entire society might have arrived more quickly at something approaching a consensus in favor of equal rights for women.

RE-CREATE THE NATION
The Religious Right and the Abortion Myth

The Religious Right's most cherished and durable myth is its myth of origins. According to this well-rehearsed narrative, articulated by Jerry Falwell, Pat Robertson, and countless others, evangelical leaders were shaken out of their political complacency by the U.S. Supreme Court's *Roe v. Wade* decision of January 22, 1973. Falwell even recounted, albeit fourteen years later, his horror at reading the news in the January 23, 1973, edition of the *Lynchburg News*. "The Supreme Court had just made a decision by a seven-to-two margin that would legalize the killing of millions of unborn children," Falwell wrote. "I sat there staring at the *Roe v. Wade* story, growing more and more fearful of the consequences of the Supreme Court's act and wondering why so few voices had been raised against it." The myth of origins has Falwell and other evangelical leaders emerging like a mollusk out of their apolitical stupor to fight the moral outrage of legalized abortion. Some even went so far as to invoke the moniker "new abolitionists" in an effort to ally themselves with their antebellum evangelical predecessors who sought to eradicate the scourge of slavery.[1]

The abortion myth, however, collapses in the face of historical scrutiny. In 1970 the United Methodist Church General Conference called on state legislatures to repeal laws restricting abortion, and in 1972, the same gathering that Jimmy Carter addressed as governor, the Methodists acknowledged "the sanctity of unborn human life" but also declared that "we are equally bound to respect the sacredness of the life and well-being of the mother, for whom devastating damage may result from unacceptable pregnancy." Meeting in St. Louis during the summer of 1971, the messengers (delegates) to the Southern Baptist Convention passed a resolution that stated, "we call upon Southern Baptists to work for legislation that will allow the possibility of abortion under such conditions as rape, incest, clear evidence of severe fetal deformity, and carefully ascertained evidence of the likelihood of damage to the emotional, mental, and physical health of the mother." The Southern Baptist Convention, hardly a redoubt of liberalism, reaffirmed that position in 1974, the year after the *Roe* decision, and again in 1976.[2]

When the *Roe* decision was handed down, W. A. Criswell, former president of the Southern Baptist Convention and pastor of First Baptist Church in Dallas, Texas, expressed his satisfaction with the ruling. "I have always felt that it was only after a child was born and had a life separate from its mother that it became an individual person," one of the most famous fundamentalists of the twentieth century declared, "and it has always, therefore, seemed to me that what is best for the mother and for the future should be allowed."[3]

While a few evangelical voices, including *Christianity Today* magazine, mildly criticized the ruling, the overwhelming response on the part of evangelicals was silence, even approval; Baptists, in particular, applauded the decision as an appropriate articulation of the line of division between church and state, between personal morality and state regulation of individual behavior. "Religious liberty, human equality and justice are advanced by the Supreme Court abortion decision," W. Barry Garrett of *Baptist Press* wrote. Floyd Robertson of the National Association of Evangelicals disagreed with the *Roe* decision, but he believed that legal redress should not be a priority for evangelicals. "The abortion issue should also remind evangelicals that the church must never rely on the state to support its mission or enforce its moral standards," he wrote in the summer 1973 issue of the organization's newsletter, *United Evangelical Action*. "The church and state must be separate. The actions and conduct of Christians transcend the secular community for which the state is responsible."[4]

The real origins of the Religious Right are rather more prosaic and less high-minded. In May 1969 a group of African American parents in Holmes County, Mississippi, filed suit to prevent three new whites-only academies from securing tax exemption from the Internal Revenue Service (IRS); each of the schools had been founded to evade desegregation of the public schools. In Holmes County the number of white students enrolled in the public schools had dropped from 771 to 28 during the first year of desegregation; the following year, that number fell to zero. The court case, known as *Green v. Kennedy*, won a temporary injunction against the "segregation academies" in January 1970, and later that year Richard Nixon ordered the IRS to enact a new policy that would deny tax exemptions to segregated schools. In July 1970 the IRS announced that, in accordance with the provisions of the Civil Rights Act of 1964, which forbade racial segregation and discrimination, it would no longer grant tax-exempt status to private schools with racially discriminatory policies. Such institutions were not—by definition—charitable organizations, and therefore they had no claims to tax-exempt status; similarly, donations to such organizations would no longer qualify as tax-deductible contributions. On November 30, 1970, the IRS sent letters of inquiry to schools in question in an effort to ascertain whether or not they discriminated on the basis of race. Bob Jones University, a fundamentalist school in Greenville, South Carolina, responded that it did not admit African Americans.[5]

Meanwhile, the *Green v. Kennedy* suit was joined with a similar suit to become *Green v. Connally*. On June 30, 1971, the U.S. District Court for the District of Columbia issued its ruling in the *Green v. Connally* case: "Under the Internal Revenue Code, properly construed, racially discriminatory private schools are not entitled to the Federal tax exemption provided for charitable, educational institutions, and persons making gifts to such schools are not entitled to the deductions provided in case of gifts to charitable, educational institutions."[6]

Paul Weyrich, who became the architect of the Religious Right, saw his opening. Ever since Barry Goldwater's campaign for the presidency in 1964, Weyrich had been trying to organize evangelicals politically. Their numbers alone, he reasoned, would constitute a formidable voting bloc, and he aspired to marshal them behind conservative causes. "The new political philosophy must be defined by us in moral terms, packaged in non-religious language, and propagated throughout the country by our new coalition," Weyrich wrote in spelling out his vision. "When political power is achieved, the moral majority will have the opportunity to re-create this great nation." Weyrich believed that the political possibilities of such a coalition were unlimited. "The leadership, moral philosophy, and workable vehicle are at hand just waiting to be blended and activated," he wrote. "If the moral majority acts, results could well exceed our wildest dreams."[7]

But Weyrich's dreams, still a hypothetical coalition that he already referred to as "moral majority" (lowercase letters), needed a catalyst—not simply an event or issue that would ignite all the indignation that had been accumulating, but also a standard around which to rally. For nearly two decades, Weyrich, by his own account, had tried various issues to pique evangelical interest in his scheme, including pornography, school prayer, the proposed Equal Rights Amendment to the Constitution, and abortion. "I was trying to get these people interested in those issues and I utterly failed," Weyrich recalled in 1990. "What changed their mind was Jimmy Carter's intervention against the Christian schools, trying to deny them tax-exempt status on the basis of so-called de facto segregation."[8]

Because the *Green v. Connally* ruling was "applicable to all private schools in the United States at all levels of education," Bob Jones University stood directly in the IRS crosshairs. Founded in Florida by archfundamentalist Bob Jones in 1926, the school had been located for a time in Cleveland, Tennessee, before moving to South Carolina in 1947. In response to *Green v. Connally*, Bob Jones University admitted a married black man, a worker in the school's radio station, as a part-time student. He dropped out a month later. Out of fears of racial mixing, the school maintained its restrictions against admitting unmarried African Americans until 1975. Even then, however, the school stipulated that interracial dating would be grounds for expulsion, and the school also promised that any students who "espouse, promote, or encourage others to violate the University's dating rules and regulations will be expelled."[9]

The IRS pursued its case against Bob Jones University and on April 16, 1975, notified the school of the proposed revocation of its tax-exempt status. On January 19, 1976, the IRS officially revoked Bob Jones University's tax-exempt status, effective retroactively to 1971, when the school had first been formally notified of the IRS policy. As Bob Jones University sued to retain its tax exemption, Weyrich pressed his case. Evangelical leaders, especially those whose schools were affected by the ruling, were angry, construing the decision as government intrusion in religious matters. Weyrich used the *Green v. Connally* case to rally evangelicals against the government. When "the Internal Revenue Service tried to deny tax exemption to private schools," Weyrich said in an interview with *Conservative Digest*, that "more than any single act brought the fundamentalists and evangelicals into the political process."[10]

Perhaps inadvertently, in the course of the Carter administration the IRS poured fuel on the embers of evangelical resentment. Although there is no evidence to suggest that the Carter White House participated in drafting the regulations, Jerome Kurtz, the IRS commissioner, on August 22, 1978, proposed that schools founded or expanded at the time of desegregation of public schools in their locality meet a quota of minority students or certify that they operated "in good faith on a racially non-discriminatory basis." The regulations, in effect, shifted the burden of proof from the IRS to the schools. A number of evangelicals interpreted the IRS proposals as an unwarranted violation of the sanctity of their subculture, a network of alternative institutions they had constructed as a shelter from "worldliness" in the decades following the Scopes Trial of 1925. Evangelicals flooded the IRS with letters of protest, more than 125,000 in all. The proposed regulations "kicked a sleeping dog," Richard Viguerie, one of the founders of the New Right, said. "It was the episode that ignited the religious right's involvement in real politics." When *Conservative Digest* catalogued evangelical discontent with Carter in August 1979, the IRS regulations headed the list. Abortion was not mentioned.[11]

Although the IRS backed away from many of the proposals, the fires of resentment flared. "To impose student and faculty quotas on private schools is a treacherous intervention into a Constitutionally protected activity," John Ashbrook, Republican member of Congress from Ohio, wrote to Carter. "Its arbitrary formula for student and staff recruitment will place Federal bureaucrats at the helm of policy formation for private schools." Ashbrook's House colleague, Robert Dornan of California, warned that Americans "are sick and tired of unelected bureaucrats engaging in social engineering at the expense of our cherished liberties." Weyrich encouraged Robert Billings, an evangelical, to form an organization called Christian School Action as a vehicle for building on evangelical discontent, an organization Weyrich came to regard as a "tremendous asset" to his hopes for politicizing conservative evangelicals. Billings, who had earlier founded the National Christian Action Coalition to thwart what he characterized as "an attempt by the IRS to control private schools," quickly mobilized evangelical ministers. Billings later declared, "Jerome Kurtz has done more to bring Christians together than any man since the Apostle Paul." Even Anita Bryant, who had been goaded into activism by gay rights, recognized the centrality of the school issue. "I believe the day of the comfortable Christian is over," Bryant declared. "Maybe it hasn't reached everybody in the rural areas, but it's a battle in the cities to keep them from taking over and reaching private and religious schools."[12]

In ramping up for political activism, evangelicals portrayed themselves as defending what they considered the sanctity of the evangelical subculture from outside interference. Weyrich astutely picked up on those fears. "What caused the movement to surface was the federal government's moves against Christian schools," Weyrich reiterated in 1990. "This absolutely shattered the Christian community's notions that Christians could isolate themselves inside their own institutions and teach what they pleased." For agitated evangelicals, Weyrich's conservative gospel of less government suddenly struck a responsive chord. "It wasn't the abortion issue; that wasn't sufficient," Weyrich recalled. "It was the recognition that isolation simply would no longer work in this society."[13]

Although leaders of the Religious Right in later years would seek to portray their politicization as a direct response to the *Roe v. Wade* ruling of 1973, Weyrich and other organizers of the Religious Right have been emphatic in dismissing this abortion myth. *Green v. Connally* served as the catalyst, not *Roe v. Wade*. Although many evangelicals certainly felt troubled by abortion and viewed it as part of the broader problem of promiscuity in American society, most of them regarded it as a "Catholic issue" in the realm of politics until the late 1970s. (Falwell acknowledged as much when he preached out against abortion for the first time on February 26, 1978, from his pulpit at Thomas Road Baptist Church.) Evangelical leaders, prodded by Weyrich, chose to interpret the IRS ruling against segregationist schools as an assault on the integrity and the sanctity of the evangelical subculture, ignoring the fact that exemption from taxes is itself a form of public subsidy. And that is what prompted them to action and to organize into a political movement. "What caused the movement to surface," Weyrich reiterated, "was the federal government's moves against Christian schools," which, he added, "enraged the Christian community."[14]

Ed Dobson, formerly Falwell's assistant at Moral Majority, corroborated Weyrich's account. "The Religious New Right did not start because of a concern about abortion," he said in 1990. "I sat in the non-smoke-filled back room with the Moral Majority, and I frankly do not remember abortion being mentioned as a reason why we ought to do something." More recently, still another conservative activist, Grover Norquist, has confirmed that the *Roe v. Wade* decision did not factor into the rise of the Religious Right. "The religious right did not get started in 1962 with prayer in school," Norquist told Dan Gilgoff, of *U.S. News & World Report*, in June 2009. "And it didn't get started in '73 with *Roe v. Wade*. It started in '77 or '78 with the Carter administration's attack on Christian schools and radio stations. That's where all of the organization flowed out of. It was complete self-defense."[15]

The actions of the IRS especially affected Bob Jones University, goading those associated with the school into political activism. Elmer L. Rumminger, longtime administrator at the university who became politically active in 1980, remembered that the IRS case "alerted the Christian school community about what could happen with government interference" in the affairs of evangelical institutions. "That was really the major issue that got us all involved to begin with—at least it was for me." What about abortion? "No, no, that wasn't the issue," he said emphatically. "This wasn't an anti-abortion movement per se. That was one of the issues we were interested in. I'm sure some people pointed to *Roe v. Wade*, but that's not what got us going. For me it was government intrusion into private education."[16]

The IRS pursuit of Bob Jones University and other schools may have captured the attention of evangelical leaders, but Weyrich was clever enough to realize that the political mobilization of evangelical and fundamentalist leaders represented only half of the equation. Unless these leaders could enlist rank-and-file evangelicals, Weyrich's dream of a politically conservative coalition of evangelicals would remain unfulfilled. And here is where abortion finally figures into the narrative.

In the 1978 midterm elections, the Democratic Party suffered a net loss of three seats in the Senate and fifteen seats in the House of

Representatives. Though not unexpected for the party in power—Republicans suffered far greater losses in the previous midterm election year of 1974, the year of Nixon's resignation—those reading the election returns could see that abortion had the potential to emerge as a political issue.

In Iowa, for example, polls and pundits expected that the incumbent Democratic senator, Richard C. "Dick" Clark, would coast easily to reelection; no poll heading into the November balloting indicated that Clark held a lead of fewer than ten percentage points. Six years earlier, Clark had walked across the state to call attention to his grassroots, upstart challenge to Jack Miller, the two-term Republican incumbent, and Clark prevailed with 55 percent of the vote. He remained a popular figure in the state. Pro-life activists, however, had targeted Clark, and on the final weekend of Clark's reelection campaign, opponents of abortion (predominantly Roman Catholics) distributed approximately three hundred thousand pamphlets in church parking lots. Two days later, in an election with very low turnout, Roger Jepsen, the Republican pro-life challenger, defeated Clark. An Election Day survey by the *Des Moines Register* indicated that about twenty-five thousand Iowans voted for Jepsen because of his stand on abortion. "I personally believe that the abortion issue was the central issue," Clark told Bruce Morton of CBS News. The senator's campaign manager agreed. "It comes right down to those leaflets they put out," he said.[17]

Christianity Today noted Clark's unexpected defeat, and the magazine also credited pro-lifers for the Republican trifecta in Minnesota, where Republican candidates who opposed abortion captured both Senate seats (one for the unexpired term of Hubert Humphrey) and the office of governor. "Anti-abortionists figured in the collapse of Minnesota's liberal Democratic-Farmer-Labor Party," the magazine reported, adding that the campaign of Albert Quie, the governor-elect and ally of Charles Colson, "distributed 250,000 leaflets to churchgoers throughout the state on the Sunday before election day."[18]

None of this was lost on Paul Weyrich. Earlier that year, Weyrich, head of the Committee for the Survival of a Free Congress, had received a check in the amount of twenty-five dollars from Georgia G. Glassman, of Gravity, Iowa. "Please make Good use of the proceeds," she wrote; "as soon as we hear that a good Republican, a Lawyer I hope, has announced his candidacy for the U.S. Senate, we Republicans will try to 'Hang Sen. Dick Clark on a telephone pole!'"[19]

Weyrich could barely contain his delight with the 1978 election returns, especially the Senate elections in Iowa and in New Hampshire, where Gordon Humphrey had ousted Thomas J. McIntyre, another Democratic incumbent. "The election of Roger Jepsen and Gordon Humphrey to the U.S. Senate is true cause for celebration, especially in view of the fact that two of the most liberal senators went down to defeat," Weyrich wrote. Even more notable, however, was how it happened: with the support of politically conservative evangelicals. Weyrich immediately set about fortifying the nascent coalition. On December 5, just a month after the election, Weyrich brought Humphrey, the senator-elect from New Hampshire, and his wife to a gathering of evangelical activists. The following day, Robert Billings penned an exultant letter to Weyrich, praising him for his "wise remarks" and congratulating him on the "smashing success" of an evening. "Paul, we did something that no-one has done in years—we brought together the three main factions of the fundamentalist community," Billings wrote. "I believe something was started last night that will pull together many of our 'fringe' Christian friends." Billings concluded his handwritten letter, "Thank you for your important part. God bless you!"[20]

The 1978 election provided the opening that Weyrich had been seeking. The previous year Weyrich had appealed to the head of the Republican National Committee to court evangelical and fundamentalist voters, but the appeal fell on deaf ears; the chair of the committee "didn't understand what I was talking about," Weyrich said, "It was so foreign to him that it didn't make any sense." Undeterred, Weyrich resolved to "go out and elect some improbable people in the

'78 elections." Although Weyrich highlighted the schools issue, the defeat of Dick Clark in Iowa and the triple win for pro-life Republicans in Minnesota suggested that abortion might very well be the issue that would galvanize grassroots evangelicals and fundamentalists into a cohesive political movement. Recall Robert Billings' letter to Weyrich a month after the midterm elections: "Paul, we did something that no-one has done in years—we brought together the three main factions of the fundamentalist community."[21]

In persuading evangelicals that abortion was a moral issue that demanded their political activism, Weyrich received help from an unlikely source, a goateed, knicker-wearing philosopher and Presbyterian minister, Francis A. Schaeffer, who, together with his wife, ran a community and study center in Switzerland. Schaeffer, considered by many the intellectual godfather of the Religious Right, began to weigh in about the pervasiveness of what he called "secular humanism" in American society. He lamented the loss of "basically a Christian consensus" and said that "we now live in a secularized society."[22]

By the late 1970s, Schaeffer was beginning to cite abortion as one consequence of a troubling cultural shift away from the mores of evangelical Christianity and toward the reviled secular humanism. Schaeffer viewed abortion as the inevitable prelude to infanticide and euthanasia, and he wanted to sound the alarm. When Schaeffer visited Fulton J. Sheen, the famous Roman Catholic bishop, in the late 1970s, Sheen applauded Schaeffer for his attempts to engage Protestants on the abortion issue. "The problem is," Sheen said, "that abortion is perceived as a Catholic issue. I want you to help me change that." Schaeffer did so through his writings and lectures, but he also teamed with C. Everett Koop, a pediatric surgeon, to produce a series of five films, collectively titled *Whatever Happened to the Human Race?* These films, produced by Billy Zeoli, Gerald Ford's religious adviser, financed in part by Richard De Vos of Amway, and directed by Schaeffer's son, Frank, found a wide audience among evangelicals when they appeared in 1978. Although Francis Schaeffer died in 1983, and Frank Schaeffer now claims that his father was appalled at the machinations of Religious Right leaders, the films, together with a companion book by the same title, served to introduce abortion to evangelicals as a moral concern. "By the end of the *Whatever Happened to the Human Race?* tour," Frank Schaeffer recalled, "we were calling for civil disobedience, the takeover of the Republican Party, and even hinting at overthrowing our 'unjust pro-abortion government.'" Years later, Robert Maddox, Jimmy Carter's liaison for religious affairs, recounted his only encounter with Schaeffer, who was visiting the office of Alonzo McDonald, an evangelical who served as Carter's deputy chief of staff. "I think you've caused a great damage here with this abortion stuff," Maddox said. Shaeffer's quiet response, according to Maddox: "Could be."[23]

Weyrich's prescience about expanding abortion from a preponderantly "Catholic issue" into an evangelical preoccupation was nothing short of brilliant. His success in blaming Carter for the IRS action against Christian schools may also have been brilliant, but it was also mendacious because Carter bore no responsibility for that. After years of warnings, the IRS finally rescinded the tax exemption of Bob Jones University on January 19, 1976, because of its persistent racist policies. That date, January 19, 1976 was a notable one for Jimmy Carter—but not because he was in any way responsible for the action against Bob Jones University. Carter won the Iowa precinct caucuses on January 19, 1976, his first major step toward capturing the Democratic presidential nomination. He took office as president a year and a day later. Weyrich and the Religious Right, however, persuaded many evangelicals that Carter, not Gerald Ford, who was then president, was somehow responsible for this unconscionable "assault" on Christian schools. In Weyrich's words, "Jimmy Carter's intervention against the Christian schools, trying to deny them tax-exempt status on the basis of so-called de facto segregation" prompted preachers like Jerry Falwell to mobilize against him.[24]

For politically conservative evangelicals in the late 1970s, Jimmy Carter's refusal to seek a constitutional amendment banning abortion came to be seen as an unpardonable sin, despite his long-standing opposition to abortion and the efforts of his administration to limit the incidence of abortion. Carter, in fact, had a longer and more consistent record of opposing abortion than Ronald Reagan.

The 1980 presidential election would test the mettle of this new coalition crafted by the hands of Weyrich, Falwell, Billings, and others. The nascent Religious Right courted several candidates in advance of the 1980 Republican primaries, including Philip Crane and John Connally, the former governor of Texas and former secretary of the treasury. The leaders of the Religious Right settled on Reagan, despite his episodic church attendance, his divorce and remarriage, and the fact that, as governor of California in 1967, he had signed into law the most liberal abortion bill in the nation.

The politicking of the Religious Right, however, despite its unsavory origins, would help defeat Jimmy Carter, their fellow evangelical, and propel Reagan to the presidency.

9

HIS OWN RECEIVED HIM NOT
Jimmy Carter, the Religious Right, and
the 1980 Presidential Election

A s the 1980 presidential campaign reached its climax, an interested citizen, a preacher, picked up the telephone. Although the race was still fluid, his preferred candidate was trailing in the polls, and yet inserting himself explicitly into the race was dicey. His ability to sway voters, especially religious voters, was undisputed, but that influence derived precisely from his ability to appear above the fray. Over the course of a long and distinguished career, he had perfected the art of the discreet political gesture—a strategic handshake, a brief touch on the shoulder, a whispered aside in front of the cameras—to telegraph his preferences.

But this election was especially fraught. One candidate, the incumbent running for reelection, was known as a family man who shared the preacher's evangelical theological convictions almost verbatim. The other major candidate, divorced and remarried, had spent much of his career in Hollywood, a province not known to evangelicals as an outpost of piety. Still another candidate, John B. Anderson, who was mounting a third-party challenge, was a member of the Evangelical Free Church, an evangelical denomination with deep roots in Scandinavian Pietism.

Receiver in hand, the preacher considered his options one last time and punched the numbers. At the other end of the line was Paul Laxalt, U.S. senator from Nevada and national chairman of Ronald Reagan's campaign for president. A memorandum in the Reagan Library tells the remainder of the story. "Billy Graham called," the senator wrote. "Wants to help short of public endorsement." Then, Laxalt added, "His presence, in my view, would be exceedingly helpful in some of our key states."[1]

Eleven days later, Graham sent a letter to Robert L. Maddox, Jimmy Carter's religious liaison. "I wanted to discuss the religious situation and the political campaign," Graham wrote. "As you know, with the Lord's help I am staying out of it. Naturally I am losing some support from people who normally support me." Graham nevertheless sought to distinguish himself from "the extreme right-wingers who are getting a great deal of exposure right now."[2]

Graham's statement that he was "staying out of" the political campaign was, to say the least, disingenuous. Nor was this the first presidential campaign where Graham pushed the boundaries of credibility. Twenty years earlier, on August 10, 1960, Graham sent a letter to John F. Kennedy, the Democratic nominee, pledging that he would not raise the "religious issue" in the fall campaign. Eight days later, Graham convened a group of American Protestant ministers in Montreux, Switzerland, to strategize about how they might prevent Kennedy's election that November. Later in the same campaign, Graham visited Henry Luce at the Time & Life Building and, according to Graham's autobiography, said, "I want to help Nixon without blatantly endorsing him." Graham drafted an article praising Nixon that stopped just short of a full endorsement. Luce was prepared to run it in *Life* magazine but pulled it at the last minute.[3]

In 1960 eight days had elapsed between Graham's letter of assurance to Kennedy and the Montreux gathering. During the 1980 campaign, eleven days separated Graham's phone call offering help to the Republican nominee and his pledge of neutrality to a staff member of the Democratic nominee.

Although Carter was never personally close to Graham, the Carters had invited Graham and his wife, Ruth, to dinner at the White House the previous November. "For several hours, we reminisced about our southern backgrounds and talked about national affairs," Graham remembered. "We shared our mutual faith in Jesus Christ and discussed some of the issues that sometimes divide sincere Christians." The Grahams stayed overnight in the Lincoln Bedroom. "Ruth and I came away with a new insight into the dedication of both of you to the cause not only of peace and justice in the world, but evangelistic urgency," Graham wrote to the Carters in appreciation.[4]

What Carter didn't know was that just a couple of weeks earlier, Graham had convened a dozen fellow preachers in Dallas for "a special time of prayer" and talk about the upcoming presidential campaign. Carter's liaison for religious affairs had only recently returned from a visit to the evangelist's home in Montreat, North Carolina, with a report that Graham "supports the President wholeheartedly." But that support was apparently less than robust. The Dallas guest list, formulated by Graham himself, included his brother-in-law, Clayton Bell; Rex Humbard and James Robison, both of them televangelists; and a roster of well-known Southern Baptists: Charles Stanley, Jimmy Draper, and Adrian Rogers, the new president of the Southern Baptist Convention who had recently visited Carter at the White House and declared it "one of the highlights of my life." The ministers, gathered at Graham's behest, occupied nearly an entire floor of the hotel. "It really was Billy's meeting," Robison recalled. "What he wanted us to do was pray together for a couple of days and to understand something very significant had to happen." The unmistakable subtext of the gathering was the need to rally behind someone who could mount a challenge to Carter. "No one was talking about Jimmy Carter's faith," Robison said. "It was his ability to lead."[5]

Just as he had done at the Montreux gathering of Protestant ministers in 1960, Graham made it clear to the participants in Dallas that he could not be the point person for such a crusade in opposition to Carter; the evangelist was still too damaged from his associations with Richard Nixon, and he wanted—publicly, at least—to remain above the fray of politics. According to Robison, a consensus emerged "that if former California governor Ronald Reagan had the conviction that he appeared to have," he would be a good choice to displace Carter. Robison was deputized to approach the Reagan camp to ascertain how serious he was about another run for the presidency.[6]

Reagan, however, was not the only contender for evangelical sympathies; his divorce and his Hollywood pedigree made many evangelicals uneasy. Paul Weyrich, architect of the Religious Right, set up a meeting between conservative evangelical leaders and John Connally, the former Democratic governor of Texas who served as Richard Nixon's secretary of the treasury and who had changed his party affiliation to Republican in 1973. The meeting was going smoothly until one of the preachers asked Connally's views on secular humanism. No one, apparently, had briefed the former governor that the term *secular humanism* was Religious Right code language for everything amiss in America. "Well, I don't know much about it," Connally declared, "but it sounds good to me!"[7]

The leaders of the Religious Right settled on Reagan.

The story of how evangelicals abandoned one of their own during the course of Jimmy Carter's presidency remains one of the great paradoxes of American politics. Evangelicals had been largely absent from the political arena for half a century before Carter's improbable ascent to the White House. The Scopes Trial of 1925 had chastened American evangelicals and persuaded them that the larger culture was hostile to them and to their interests. In response, evangelicals, especially in the North, retreated into a subculture of their own making. They constructed an elaborate and interlocking network of congregations, denominations, Bible camps, Bible institutes, colleges, seminaries, publishing houses, and mission societies—all of them inward looking, a defensive bulwark against the temptations and depredations of the larger culture.

Evangelicals associated politics with that culture, and any impulses they might have harbored to reform society were thwarted by premillennialism, the conviction that Jesus would return *before* the millennium predicted in the book of Revelation. That is not to say that all evangelicals were politically inactive. Although many did not vote—premillennialism inferred that this world was doomed and transitory, so why bother?—others participated in the political process, though rarely with much enthusiasm. The Cold War aversion to communism as a godless system nudged them toward the political right, the persistence of anti-Catholicism bred suspicion of John F. Kennedy and the Democratic Party, and Billy Graham's clear preference for Republican politicians, especially Dwight Eisenhower and Richard Nixon, reinforced a general sense that, for evangelicals in the North, at least, the Republican Party was the preferred alternative.

Jimmy Carter's appearance on the political scene altered that calculus. His frequent declarations that he was a "born again" Christian proved difficult to ignore, especially because the media had seized on those statements with such glee and incredulity. For evangelicals, however, he was speaking their language, and the fact that he did so openly and without shame or apology made the statements even more striking.

Carter's campaign for the presidency also built on a brief and fleeting recrudescence of progressive evangelicalism. Popular revulsion over the Vietnam War, and especially Nixon's corrupt administration, had provided an opening for progressive evangelicals like Ronald Sider and Jim Wallis. The Chicago Declaration of Evangelical Social Concern, formulated and signed by fifty-five prominent evangelicals in November 1973, sounded many of the themes that had been common among nineteenth- and early twentieth-century evangelicals: peace, nonviolence, racial reconciliation, advocacy for the rights of women, and care for those Jesus called "the least of these." Although Carter himself was unaware of the Chicago Declaration, his campaign echoed many of the same positions and harvested the support of progressive evangelicals.

Carter also sought to be the first president elected from the Deep South since the Civil War. To do so he needed to persuade the voters that he was not a racist. Despite his tawdry campaign for governor in 1970, during which he courted the support of segregationists, Carter quickly pivoted and, during his inauguration, announced that "the time for racial discrimination is over." The media promptly anointed him an avatar of the so-called New South, and Carter responded with unmistakable overtures to African Americans, including support for education and prison reform and the installation of Martin Luther King Jr.'s portrait in the Georgia statehouse. Carter burnished those credentials by vanquishing George C. Wallace, the nation's most notorious segregationist, in the 1976 Florida Democratic primary.

Having ridden this wave of progressive evangelicalism and New South capaciousness to the White House, Carter expected that the last constituency he needed to worry about was evangelicals. He was, after all, representing the best of that tradition by advocating human rights, peace in the Middle East, better, more equitable relations with Latin America, and a less imperial foreign policy. Domestically, his support for public education, racial reconciliation, and the proposed Equal Rights Amendment to the Constitution were utterly consistent with the principles of nineteenth-century evangelicalism.

So why were evangelicals preparing to abandon Jimmy Carter, one of their own, in advance of the 1980 presidential election? The short answer is that the surge of progressive evangelicalism in the 1970s proved just as evanescent as New South optimism. The longer answer has to do with the emergence of the Religious Right in the late 1970s.

The demise of Richard Nixon's troubled presidency in the early 1970s had temporarily stymied the efforts of conservative operatives to mobilize evangelical voters behind the Republican Party. That hiatus provided progressive evangelicalism with its brief opening. But strategists like Paul Weyrich, whose party activism dated back to Barry Goldwater's campaign for the presidency in 1964, refused to concede evangelical voters to Carter and the Democratic Party. What Weyrich needed, however, was an issue that would galvanize evangelical leaders, first of all, and then grassroots evangelicals. As it happened, those would be two separate issues.

According to Weyrich's own account, he recognized the electoral potential of American evangelicals early on, and he auditioned a succession of issues in the 1960s and 1970s to win their allegiance: support for prayer in schools and opposition to pornography, the Equal Rights Amendment, and abortion. Nothing worked. Then, unexpectedly, Weyrich found the issue that would motivate evangelical leaders: tax exemption.

On June 30, 1971, the district court for the District of Columbia handed down a ruling in a case called *Green v. Connally*. In that case, which involved religious, segregated schools in Mississippi, the Internal Revenue Service (IRS) had ruled that, in light of the Civil Rights Act of 1964, any institution that engages in racial discrimination is not, by definition, a charitable institution; therefore, it has no claims to tax-exempt status. The *Green v. Connally* ruling upheld the IRS, and in the ensuing years as the agency sought to enforce the ruling, one of the institutions they targeted was a fundamentalist school in Greenville, South Carolina. Bob Jones University did not admit African Americans until 1971 and, out of fears of racial mixing, did not admit unmarried African Americans until 1975. When, after years of warnings, the IRS rescinded Bob Jones University's tax exemption on January 19, 1976, Weyrich finally had the issue that would motivate evangelical leaders. He whipped up the outrage— and managed somehow to direct the fury at Jimmy Carter, despite the fact that the day Bob Jones University lost its tax exemption— January 19, 1976—Carter was winning the Iowa precinct caucuses and was not yet even close to capturing the Democratic nomination. That made little difference to Weyrich or to the growing ranks of aggrieved evangelical leaders. Jerry Falwell, who had criticized the

Brown v. Board of Education ruling of 1954 and had opened his own segregation academy in the 1960s, famously remarked that it was easier
to open a massage parlor in most states than a "Christian" school.

Enlisting evangelical leaders was one thing, but finding an issue
that would mobilize the grassroots was another. When Weyrich
finally stumbled onto the abortion issue in the midterm elections
of 1978, he solved the riddle of the evangelical vote. Ironically, the
Reagan-Bush campaign was slow to catch on. At a rally of fifteen
thousand evangelicals at Reunion Arena in Dallas on August 22,
1980, Reagan endorsed creationism and railed against the Carter
administration for rescinding tax-exempt status for segregation
academies. He said that if he were stranded on an island and could
have only one book, that book would be the Bible. The Republican
nominee, however, never mentioned abortion.

Carter faced a daunting challenge in his run for a second term in
1980: a sagging economy, the Soviet invasion of Afghanistan, the
taking of American hostages in Iran, a primary challenge within his
own party. But he was also blindsided by the defection of his fellow
evangelicals, who had helped elect him four years earlier. Carter said
he first became aware of evangelical discontent when his sister, Ruth
Carter Stapleton, a pentecostal evangelist, informed him that Jerry
Falwell was saying all sorts of nasty things about the president up in
Juneau, Alaska, part of Falwell's tour of state capitols to drum up
opposition to Carter in advance of the 1980 election. The president
knew he was in trouble when conservatives mounted a takeover of
the Southern Baptist Convention, Carter's own denomination, in
June 1979. Following that gathering, a delegation of the church's
new leaders visited the White House. At the conclusion of the meeting, Bailey Smith told Carter, "We are praying, Mr. President, that
you will abandon secular humanism as your religion." The president
later recorded that when he returned to the family quarters that evening, he asked Rosalynn, "What's a secular humanist?"[8]

Progressive evangelicals, who had contributed to Carter's electoral coalition in 1976, stayed on the sidelines in 1980; John Alexander, editor of *The Other Side*, suggested that his readers vote for Donald Duck. Under the tutelage of operatives like Paul Weyrich, on the other hand, the Religious Right had fashioned a formidable political machine, which they used to deny one of their own, Jimmy Carter, a second term as president.

The political career of Jimmy Carter is riddled with paradox and contradiction. The man who ran a race-baiting campaign for governor in 1970 quickly repented and became a champion of racial reconciliation and the principles of progressive evangelicalism. He lured other evangelicals into the political arena in 1976, but many of those same evangelicals turned rabidly against him four years later in favor of a divorced and remarried former Hollywood actor who, as governor of California, had signed into law one of the most liberal abortion laws in the nation.

Paradoxes aplenty. Although Carter himself would never countenance messianic parallels, the words of the Gospel of John are appropriate. He came unto his own in 1976, but by 1980 his own received him not.

10

KEEP THE FAITH AND GO THE DISTANCE
Promise Keepers, Feminism, and the World of Sports

Throughout church history, dating back to the New Testament, Christians have used two metaphors for spirituality: militarism and athleticism. St. Paul admonished the early Christians to run the race and to put on the full armor of God in their battle against the wiles of the devil. These metaphors have been played out in various ways across the centuries. The monks were spiritual athletes of a sort, training in godliness and implicitly competing with one another in the quest for holiness. The Crusades provided a religious legitimacy—and absolution—for military conquest, and the Society of Jesus was mobilized explicitly as the pope's army.

In American history the military metaphor dominated nineteenth- and early twentieth-century piety. It took various organizational forms—the Salvation Army, the Knights of Columbus, Awana Clubs, Christian Service Brigade, and Campus Crusade for Christ—but it also pervaded evangelical hymnody, as suggested by "Onward Christian Soldiers," "We're Marching to Zion," and "Rise Up, O Men of God."

Both the military and the athletic metaphors were especially appealing to men and were appropriated shamelessly in the muscular Christianity movement, which combined seduction and taunting in roughly equal parts. At the turn of the twentieth century, Billy Sunday, formerly a baseball player for the Chicago White Stockings, cajoled the men in his audiences to "hit the sawdust trail" and give their lives to Jesus. "Many think a Christian has to be a sort of dishrag proposition, a wishy-washy, sissified sort of galoot that lets everybody make a doormat out of him," Sunday intoned. "Let me tell you the manliest man is the man who will acknowledge Jesus Christ." A few years later, at about the same time that Charles Sheldon's novel *In His Steps* portrayed Jesus as an astute businessman, an organization called the Men and Religion Forward Movement summoned men back to the churches with the slogan "More Men for Religion, More Religion for Men." The campaign held rallies in places like Carnegie Hall, rented billboards on Times Square, and placed display ads in the sports sections of newspapers.[1]

Immediately after World War II, muscular Christianity drew more heavily on the militarism metaphor, but the athletic ideal was never entirely absent. James C. Hefley published edifying biographical sketches of professional athletes who professed to be Christians: Bobby Richardson, Dave Wickersham, Bill Glass, Al Worthington, among many others. The movement encompassed such organizations as Athletes in Action (a subsidiary of Campus Crusade for Christ, thereby combining the motifs of militarism and athleticism), the Fellowship of Christian Athletes, and Power Team for Christ, a weightlifting troupe that travels to various venues and intersperses evangelistic testimonies with spectacular feats of strength.[2]

In more recent years, athletics has gradually eclipsed militarism as the predominant metaphor for evangelical spirituality. The Vietnam War dimmed somewhat our collective enthusiasm for the military. Even Ralph Reed, executive director of Christian Coalition, claims to have eschewed militaristic rhetoric. "Early in the 1990s, I occasionally used military metaphors for effect," he wrote in 1996, but Reed recognized the perils of such language and "sent out a memorandum to our grassroots leaders urging them to avoid military rhetoric and to use sports metaphors instead." It should come as no surprise, then, that Promise Keepers, the muscular Christianity of the 1990s, should be suffused with the accoutrements of athleticism. Bill McCartney, the founder of Promise Keepers, was a highly successful football coach who led the University of Colorado Buffaloes from obscurity to national rankings and the Associated Press National Championship in 1990. McCartney's rhetoric sometimes veers toward militarism—as when he declares, "We're in a war, men, whether we like it or not"—but Promise Keepers rallies and publications most often feature athletes, and the gatherings themselves take place in sports arenas.[3]

By the mid-1990s, the media had become inured to the specter of large stadiums filled with men praying, chanting, and singing at the top of their lungs, many with their arms outstretched in that familiar pentecostal gesture of openness to the Holy Spirit. Promise Keepers, the latest incarnation of the muscular Christianity impulse in American history, traces its origins to an automobile trip between Boulder and Pueblo, Colorado. On March 20, 1990, McCartney, then the head football coach at Colorado, and his friend Dave Wardell were traveling to a meeting of the Fellowship of Christian Athletes in Pueblo, and in the course of their conversation, they came upon the idea of filling Colorado's Folsom Stadium with men dedicated to the notion of Christian discipleship. This vision spread to a cohort of seventy-two men, who engaged in fasting and prayer in support of the notion.

Over four thousand men showed up for the first gathering, and by July 1993 McCartney's original vision had been fulfilled: fifty thousand men piled into Folsom Stadium for singing, hugging, and exhortations to be good and faithful husbands, fathers, and churchgoers. The organization, Promise Keepers, grew to an annual budget in excess of $100 million and offices in thirty-eight states. In 1996 more than one million men attended twenty-two rallies at stadiums across the country.[4]

The venue is significant. The sports arena in particular and sports in general are manifestations of a subculture no less than the subculture of American evangelicalism, the most important social, religious, and cultural movement in American history. The evangelical subculture was constructed in earnest during the half century between the Scopes Trial and Jimmy Carter's campaign for the presidency. It provided a place of refuge for beleaguered Protestants who felt alienated from the larger culture. Evangelicals, disturbed by the social and intellectual currents in the broader world, constructed their own universe as a refuge.

The evangelical subculture was marked by a fortress mentality, and in many ways it was more than a subculture; it was a counterculture, in that it defined itself against the prevailing norms of the larger culture. It had its own rules and customs and standards. Whereas the broader culture was enamored of "modernist" ideas in science, theology, and culture, evangelicals stubbornly clung to "orthodox" understandings of Protestant Christianity, including the virgin birth, the inerrancy of the Bible, and the authenticity of miracles. When flappers were all the rage in the 1920s, evangelicals placed all manner of behavioral and sartorial standards—including proscriptions on the use of jewelry and cosmetics—on their wives and daughters in order to shield them from the corrosive influences of "the world."[5]

One element of the larger culture especially did not sit well with evangelicals: feminism. It is no secret that, despite evangelicalism's noble heritage of activism on women's concerns in the nineteenth century, feminist sensibilities did not flourish within twentieth-century American evangelicalism. The women's movement and the concomitant sexual revolution threatened evangelical mores, and evangelical leaders (an overwhelmingly male cohort) responded with determined attempts to reassert the mythical ideal of feminine spirituality and domesticity. Evangelicals have blamed feminism for abortion, the rising divorce rate, the proliferation of sexually transmitted diseases, low test scores, and a general moral decline in the country. A number of evangelical organizations were formed, notably Focus on the Family and Concerned Women for America, to counteract and to reverse the tide of feminism in the United States.[6]

Here, on the issue of feminism—or, more precisely, in opposition to feminism—the subculture of sports and the evangelical sub-culture, as manifest in the Promise Keepers movement, intersect like circles on a Venn diagram. The passion for organized sports in recent years has surged at the same time that there has been a growing political discontent, especially within the middle class. This so-called "white rage" fueled the political ambitions of Ross Perot in 1992, and it helped to sustain Pat Buchanan's seemingly endless campaign for the presidency during the 1990s. The contours of this discontent, rehearsed endlessly on talk radio, have been amply documented, but Thomas L. Friedman's column on the op-ed page of the *New York Times* during the 1996 presidential primaries provides a useful summary. "If the economy is doing so well," Friedman asked rhetorically on behalf of his readers, "why have I just been downsized out of a job and why do I feel like my community is eroding?" Friedman and others referred to this as the politics of resentment, and its symptoms are that "our schools no longer teach right from wrong, that our nation can't control its borders and that patriotism is giving way to multiculturalism."[7]

The world, in short, is out of control. This politics of resentment, when articulated by other oracles, has located different demons. In the past it has fingered communism and the United Nations; more recent targets include the North American Free Trade Agreement (NAFTA), foreign aid, welfare, affirmative action, Hillary Rodham Clinton, and, more generally, feminism.[8]

Feminism. One of the most far-reaching social revolutions in American history began in 1963 with the publication of *The Feminine Mystique* by Betty Friedan. The women's movement brought radical changes in gender roles, economic expectations, sexual behavior, the composition of families, and language. In 1945 the number of American women in the labor force stood at 29 percent; by 1970 that number rose to 38 percent, and in 1995 to

46 percent. Women have not been content to stay at home, and, despite the well-publicized glass ceiling, they have entered every arena of American life, from the military to the Supreme Court, from the picket lines to the corporate boardroom.[9]

Every arena of American life, save one: the sports arena. In spite of Title IX provisions, women's athletics still lags behind men's, and in the realm of professional sports, women are virtually nonexistent, aside from golf and tennis and a struggling basketball league. Even though the San Diego Clippers drafted Iowa basketball whiz Denise Long some years ago, and every so often you read of a female referee or umpire aspiring to make it into the major leagues, women have not been able, for the most part, to break into the male preserve of professional team sports.

The venue for Promise Keepers rallies underscores the sympathies between sports and spirituality. The world of athletics offers an alternative universe, a subculture that provides a refuge from the larger world. In contrast to that larger world, the world of sports is an orderly universe. This, of course, is not a new observation. In every major sport, the ball represents the world; when the ball stops, play itself stops. In football, which is essentially a military game concerned with the capture and defense of territory, the movement of the ball signals the beginning of play. Basketball, an urban game invented by a YMCA secretary in Springfield, Massachusetts, mimics the urban landscape in that it demands that players maneuver within very narrow confines, similar to the urban world itself. Baseball, the only game in which the defense controls the ball, is a game developed and played by immigrants, and it perfectly mirrored their own world. In baseball the batter is outnumbered nine to one in his attempt to disrupt the defense's control of the world. The defense is malevolently effective most of the time, and anyone who is successful three times out of ten will probably find a place someday in the Hall of Fame. For the batter, as for the immigrant, the greatest—and most elusive—triumph is to return home, but it is a journey fraught with perils and very few islands of safety along the way.

McCartney's affinity with football, as opposed to baseball or other sports, merely underscores the sense of beleaguerment claimed by evangelical males. From its earliest origins in the bastions of privilege of the Northeast, football was unabashedly militaristic. One early enthusiast equated the brutality of warfare with the violence of football. "War," according to John Prentiss Jr., a fullback, "is the greatest game on earth." Whereas baseball, the game of immigrants engaged in an overwhelming struggle against stiff odds, represented a view of America from the bottom up, football, a game of brute force and relentless domination, offered an elite vision. The big three football powerhouses at the turn of the century—Yale, Princeton, and Harvard—imposed their will on opponents, sometimes racking up scores in triple digits.[10]

What all major sports have in common since the age of industrialism are clear boundaries and precise delineations. The rules may be complex, but they too are precise, with every situation and contingency provided for. Something is either in bounds or out of bounds, safe or out, fair or foul. The only thing that can disrupt this orderly universe is a misjudgment. Nothing enrages a sports devotee more than a bad call from an official, whose job is to act as an impartial judge and a benign authority figure. The official has no prerogative to be a judicial activist. He cannot hear mitigating arguments before rendering his judgment. A batter thrown out by a step at first base, for example, cannot argue that he should be called safe because, had he not injured his ankle back in spring training, he would almost certainly have beaten the throw from shortstop and that to call him out on that play betrayed the umpire's bias against players who are in some way disabled. The wide receiver who failed to plant both feet in bounds before falling out of the end zone cannot argue that he simply forgot to do so and that such negligence should not be held against him and that, furthermore, any adverse ruling would unfairly punish the entire team for the inadvertent lapse of one of its players. No, the officials must render simple, impartial judgments lest they violate the orderly universe that is the world of sports.[11]

If the domain of sports provides an alternative, male-dominated universe where the voices of women rarely intrude, the same can be said of Promise Keepers. Women were not allowed at Promise Keepers rallies because, the organization said rather vaguely, "the conferences are designed for specific men's issues in the context of an all-male setting." Women, they added, serve in a supportive capacity: "There are many women volunteers praying and working behind the scenes to ensure that these events go smoothly. One of the primary goals of the conference is to deepen the commitment of men to respect and honor women."[12]

Indeed, Promise Keepers, which won a ringing endorsement from Beverly LaHaye, president of Concerned Women for America, had a great deal to say about men and their relationships with women. Promise number four (of seven) reads, "A Promise Keeper is committed to building strong marriages and families through love, protection and Biblical values." It would be difficult to gainsay the importance of such a sentiment, and if the Promise Keepers movement succeeds in encouraging men to be more attentive to their wives, to visit museums with their sons, and to take their daughters fly-fishing, it will have served a useful purpose. Part of the appeal of Promise Keepers is that it reassigns men to the private sphere in addition to the public sphere. But the ideology surrounding Promise Keepers, with its paradoxical pairing of the soft-breasted male with its reassertion of patriarchalism, refuses to acknowledge the corollary—that women can find their niche in the workplace as well as the home. Since the emergence of the cult of domesticity in the nineteenth century, women have, evangelicals believe, been the spiritual guardians of the home and are not to engage in the male-dominated public sphere. This essentialist ideal of femininity, so desperately nurtured by the leaders of evangelicalism in the twentieth century, demanded that women stay home and remain submissive to their husbands.

In *Seven Promises of a Promise Keeper*, for example, the manifesto of the movement, Gary Smalley cites the case of the Brawner family, who live in a small town in Missouri. They have a son, described as "a national swimming champion and a freshman in college," a "17-year-old who's an outstanding three-sport athlete in high school," and Jill, "their beautiful and talented 13-year-old." That description itself is revealing: the sons are athletes—successful athletes—and the daughter is "beautiful and talented." Smalley goes on to describe the return of the eldest son from college and the potential for family tension because of an earring in one ear, part of his initiation to the college swim team. Mom, who is clearly a stay-at-home mother, meets him at the door, and after a brief exchange they wonder how Dad will greet this development when he returns from work. (After a moment of suspense, Dad, it turns out, newly attuned to the demands of family life, manages to keep his temper.)[13]

What is the role of men in the domestic sphere? After decrying "the feminization of the American male," which has "produced a nation of 'sissified' men who abdicate their role as spiritually pure leaders," Tony Evans, an African American preacher who also served as chaplain to the Dallas Cowboys, makes it clear that it is "proper—in fact, essential—for children to be nurtured, guided, and cared for by women." But the man must, in Evans' words, reclaim his manhood and take charge of the household. "The first thing you do," he writes, "is sit down with your wife and say something like this: 'Honey, I've made a terrible mistake. I've given you my role. I gave up leading this family, and I forced you to take my place. Now I must reclaim that role.'" Evans insists that this is not a matter for negotiation. "Don't misunderstand what I'm saying here," he writes. "I'm not suggesting that you *ask* for your role back, I'm urging you to *take* it back."[14]

There can be little question that masculinity was a protean notion in the latter decades of the twentieth century. Promise Keepers represented an intriguing response to that malleability, an impulse to impose order on a world widely perceived as chaotic and to provide identity, direction, and solidarity for a cohort of white, evangelical, middle-class men. Much was made of the male bonding that takes place at Promise Keepers rallies, but even that might be understood in the context of militarism and athleticism.

For the older generation of American males in the 1990s, military service in World War II and the Korean War provided the venue for bonding with other men. Strong ties of friendship and camaraderie were forged in bunkers, in air squadrons, or on board a destroyer. Many in the baby boom generation, which came of age in the sixties, sought to avoid the draft, so they have no regiment reunions to show for their friendships; they do not gather in VFW halls to swap war stories and renew ties with their war buddies.

The stories of this younger generation are stories of athletic prowess: the improbable touchdown pass, the no-hitter, Steph Curry's latest improbable shot. Sports provides a common vocabulary for male interaction and bonding, so it is no accident that McCartney chose sports arenas for his gatherings or that he would pepper them with sports personalities and athletic analogies. He is simply speaking the language of the disaffected male.

Many men felt confused and angry about the women's movement—shifting gender roles, changing sexual politics and expectations from the workplace to the bedroom. For many American males, feminism was disruptive. A letter by Edward Abbey, written from "Winkelman (pop. 225 incl. dogs), Arizona," to the editors of "Mizz Magazine," merits extensive quotation as an admittedly extreme—and risible—expression of this sentiment:

> Are old wimmin is trouble enuf to manage as is without you goldam New Yorkers sneaking a lot of downright *sub-versive* ideas into their hard heads. Out here a womin's place is in the kitchen, the barnyard and the bedroom in that exackt order and we don't need no changes. We got a place for men and we got a place for wimmin and there aint no call to get them mixed up. Like my neighbor Marvin Bundy says, he says, "I seen men, I seen wimmin, I haint *never* seen one of them there *persons*. Least not in

Pinal County." Thems my sentiments too. You ladies best stick to tatting doilies. Much obliged for your kind consideration, I am

Yrs truly, Cactus Ed

The irrepressible and inimitable Abbey captured, albeit in caricature, the sentiments of many American men bewildered by the vagaries and the implications of feminism.[15]

The responses have been manifold, ranging from the primal yearnings of Robert Bly and *Iron John* to unabashed chauvinism and spousal abuse. But just as the interest in sports and sports memorabilia connotes a nostalgia for the simpler days of childhood and the quest for an orderly world, so too recent evangelical preachments about gender roles and so-called family values seek to impose an order on what they perceive as the chaos created by feminism. What the world of sports and the evangelically inspired Promise Keepers movement have in common goes beyond the mere fixation with athleticism, where the criterion for superiority is usually physical strength, and where men, therefore, can still dominate women. Promise Keepers, wittingly or not, tapped into a symbolic world that resonates with American males late in the twentieth century. Both the athletic and the military metaphors, moreover, point to dualistic views of the world; on the athletic field as on the battlefield, with rare exceptions, there are winners and losers, and evangelicals' penchant for dualism in the twentieth century has been amply documented. McCartney, drawing on male—specifically, white male—anxieties, marshaled the traditional Christian metaphors of militarism and athleticism to combat feminism, all behind the guise of a benevolent patriarchalism.[16]

Both Promise Keepers and the world of sports provide the shelter of a subculture, a contrived universe with its own standards, rules, and values. In both cases—and in contrast to the larger culture—the rules are clear and vigorously enforced. In a world perceived as disordered, these subcultures provide safety, a common language, shared assumptions, and the assurance of camaraderie.

11

DEAD STONES
The Future of American Protestantism

I have no such pretensions, but were I to offer a kind of state-of-the-union assessment of American Protestantism early in the twenty-first century, I could not be sanguine. Mainline (generally liberal) Protestantism has been ravaged by ecumenism and suffers from an appalling lack of leadership. Evangelicals, on the other hand, have a lot of shrill voices who claim to be leaders, but they represent a narrow slice of American evangelicalism; and there are few apparent leaders in the younger generation. Finally, American Protestantism is imperiled—and the republic itself arguably suffers—from the massive disappearance of Baptists from the American landscape.

Let's start with the numbers. By almost any index—attendance, membership, giving—the denominations that comprise what was traditionally known as mainline Protestantism have been in freefall since the mid-1960s. During this same span of time, these denominations have pursued the chimera of ecumenism, the blurring of theological and confessional differences in the name of Christian unity. Although I acknowledge the contribution of ecumenism in bringing comity to interdenominational relations, I've long held theological reservations about the ecumenical movement. I don't pretend to be a biblical scholar, but it seems to me at least arguable that mainline Protestants have misinterpreted the foundational text for ecumenism: Jesus' hopeful statement, recorded in John 17, that his followers "may all be one." This, I believe, was wishful thinking. Jesus was speaking eschatologically; the verb mood is subjunctive, not hortative. Yes, his followers will all be one—but not in this world, where, to quote St. Paul, "we know in part, and we prophesy in part." In the first letter to the Corinthians, moreover, Paul acknowledged that "some follow Paul and some follow Apollos," a passage that suggests to me a kind of nascent denominationalism as early as the first century.[1]

The other reason to be suspicious of ecumenism is that it has led to theological reductionism into the lowest common denominator of agreement. Put another way (with only modest hyperbole), mainline Protestants over the past several decades have traded the Holy Trinity—Father, Son, and Holy Spirit—for the "unholy trinity," usually expressed as peace, justice, and inclusiveness, or some variant thereof. Let me hasten to add that, despite my offhanded use of the term "unholy trinity," I think that peace, justice, and inclusiveness are noble ideals, ones that I affirm wholeheartedly. But there is nothing distinctively or exclusively Christian about them; my friends in the Ethical Culture movement, for instance, ardently advocate peace, justice, and inclusiveness. Individual Protestant denominations enamored of ecumenism appear ready, even eager, to discard their theological birthright in quest of the holy grail of Protestant unity. The result of this quixotic pursuit is an ideology denuded of historical reference and offering the theological nutritional value of a Twinkie.

But my larger-issue objection to ecumenism has to do with its appropriateness in the current cultural context. Historically, the most successful religious groups in American history have been exclusive rather than inclusive—consider the Methodists or the Mormons in the nineteenth century or the pentecostals in the twentieth century. The latest incarnation of the ecumenical movement was a Cold War construct, intended to present a united front against the perils of communism. The religious landscape of the United States began to change dramatically, however, after revisions to the immigration laws in 1965 opened American borders to Asians and South Asians. If nothing else, these new immigrant groups have taught us the importance of particularity as opposed to assimilation. As I've remarked many times, I've yet to jump into a taxi in New York City and have the cabbie tell me, "Yes, I'm a Hindu, but I sure have a lot to learn from those Presbyterians!"

The key to group cohesion in a multicultural context is not the elision of differences; it is rather a clear understanding of one's history, traditions, and convictions. The ecumenical movement among mainline Protestants has certainly given rise to more civility in religious discourse, and no one would dispute that that is a good thing. But in terms of numbers and cultural influence, ecumenism has been disastrous, and the failure of mainline Protestant leaders to recognize it as such suggests a stubborn, blind pursuit of failed policies as well as a disregard for the importance of doctrine.

Nothing better illustrates the appalling absence of leadership among mainline Protestants than the controversy over the election of a gay man as bishop in the Episcopal Church in 2003. At the denomination's general convention in August 2003, the presiding bishop declared that his vote in favor of confirming V. Eugene Robinson as bishop for the diocese of New Hampshire should not be construed as support for homosexuals in high ecclesiastical office. No, he insisted that his vote was merely a ratification of Robinson's election by the Episcopalians in New Hampshire. Rather than providing leadership on the issue—or, heaven forfend, offering a *theological* argument on one side of the issue or another—the presiding bishop refused to take a stand. (The archbishop of Canterbury, spiritual leader of the worldwide Anglican Communion, hardly distinguished himself either in the handling of the matter, meekly calling for a gathering of church leaders several months after Robinson's confirmation by the general convention.)

Just as disturbing as the absence of leadership is the knee-jerk reaction on both sides. Claiming fidelity to the Scriptures, conservatives opposed Robinson because of his sexual orientation, although, based on the Bible alone, they might have made a better case that Robinson was unfit for high ecclesiastical office because of his divorce; the Bible has a great deal more to say about divorce than it does about homosexuality—and we have no words whatsoever from Jesus about the matter.

Those who style themselves theological liberals, on the other hand, demonstrate a lack of discernment, and few trouble themselves to reconcile their beliefs and behavior with the teachings of Scripture. This manifests itself not only in cases like Gene Robinson, but more obviously in reckless, eclectic spirituality, one that encompasses everything from a kind of formless New Age meditation to neopaganism to Tibetan Buddhism. Although it may not bear full responsibility, the ecumenical movement, with its devaluing of theological inquiry and its least-common-denominator credo, must shoulder its share of the blame for the mindless, me-too ethic emanating from mainline Protestantism.

Evangelicalism also suffers from a crisis of leadership, but a crisis of a slightly different form. As I was addressing a gathering of presidents of several Christian colleges some time ago, the conversation came around to the greatest fear they faced in their jobs. I expected to hear about liability suits or some faculty scandal. A vote of no confidence from the faculty senate or the board of trustees should strike fear in the heart of any college president, I imagined, or the inability to balance the budget.

The answer they came up with astounded me. Their biggest fear, each of them agreed, was the possibility that James Dobson of Focus on the Family would take a dislike to their schools, for one reason or another, and use his huge media empire—radio, magazines, books—to issue a condemnation. This had happened to other schools, they assured me, and the consequences were devastating: parents refused to send their children, and donations dried up. For these presidents, the lesson was clear: don't mess with Dobson or, by extension, with any of the moguls of the Religious Right.

For more than half a century, Billy Graham set the tone for American evangelicalism. Much to his credit, and unlike many of the fundamentalists who preceded him, Graham was an irenic presence on the American religious scene. He made a self-conscious decision early in his career to break with condemnatory rhetoric and the sectarian, separatist schemes of fundamentalism in favor of cooperation with other religious leaders. The so-called Modesto Manifesto, hammered out in a meeting with his associates in a hotel room in California, included the pledge never to condemn other clergy. Some fundamentalists never forgave Graham for cooperating with the New York City Ministerial Alliance during his 1957 crusade in Madison Square Garden, but there can be little doubt that Graham's conciliatory demeanor abetted the spread of the gospel and the growth of evangelicalism. (Were he a vengeful man, which he was not, Graham could doubtless have taken satisfaction in the fact that he outlived his most vociferous fundamentalist critics: Bob Jones Jr., Jack Wyrtzen, and Carl McIntire.)

What happens to American Protestantism after Billy Graham? We are left with an array of lesser lights, none of whom possesses anywhere near the character or the stature of Graham. Even Graham's decision to pass the mantle of leadership of the Billy Graham Evangelistic Association to his son Franklin was worrisome. Franklin Graham's rhetoric suggests that, whereas his father made a decision to forsake fundamentalism in favor of evangelicalism, the son did precisely the opposite: though reared in an evangelical household, Franklin turned away from evangelicalism in favor of fundamentalism.

Is this the next generation of evangelical leaders? If so, I shudder, especially because none of them represents anything but the hard-right politics of the Religious Right, which has neglected the noble heritage of nineteenth-century evangelical activism, an activism that invariably worked on behalf of the marginalized in society: slaves, the poor, and women. Where is the next Tony Campolo or Ronald Sider or Jim Wallis? Who will replace Mark O. Hatfield, the evangelical voice of conscience in the U.S. Senate for thirty years, from 1967 until his retirement in 1997? Hatfield was arguably the last of a dying breed, a liberal Republican. When he announced that he would not run for reelection in 1996, the senator from Oregon lamented that his party, the party of Lincoln, had been commandeered by "converted Confederates." Who will stand up to the Religious Right? Why do even once-venerable evangelical publications like *Christianity Today* feel obligated repeatedly to suborn themselves to the Religious Right? Are they, too, intimidated by the evangelical right wing? If this crowd defines evangelicalism for the next generation, then I, for one, will keep my distance.

Never in my life did I think I would say this, but America suffers these days from too few Baptists. Sure, there are plenty of people who call themselves Baptists, especially in the South, where you'll find more Southern Baptists than people. But are they *really* Baptists?

The Baptist tradition in America is long and colorful and noble. Founded in America by Roger Williams, the Baptists enshrined two ideas: adult (as opposed to infant) baptism and liberty of individual conscience, generally expressed in the shorthand phrase "separation of church and state." Williams was a dissident in Puritan Massachusetts who was expelled from the colony in 1636 and went to Rhode Island to form a religiously tolerant society. It is to Williams that we owe the notion of religious disestablishment, the absence of a state church, because he saw the miserable effects of religious establishment in Massachusetts. The entanglement of church and state, Williams recognized, compromised the functions of both, although he was primarily concerned to protect the purity of the church from the intrusions of the state into religious affairs. In his words, Williams wanted to shield the "garden" of the church from the "wilderness" of the world, and, as a religious minority himself, he sought also to protect the rights of religious minorities from the government.

Williams expressed concern that any state endorsement of religion would diminish the authenticity of faith. Invoking the golden image of Daniel 2, Williams, addressing the Westminster Assembly in London in 1644, wondered if the idolatry decried by the Hebrew prophets wasn't a type "of the several national and state religions that all nations set up."[2]

The Charter of Rhode Island and Providence Plantations, granted by Charles II in 1663, enshrined Williams' Baptist principles of liberty of conscience. The people of Rhode Island aspired "to hold forth a lively experiment that a flourishing civil state may best be maintained among his Majesty's subjects with full religious liberty," the charter read, adding that "no person within the said colony shall hereafter be in any wise molested or called in question for any difference in opinion in matters of religion."[3]

In the eighteenth century, in part because of the religious pluralism in the colonies, the Baptist model of church-state separation and liberty of conscience looked more and more attractive. "It is not doubted but every man who wishes to be free will by all lawful ways in his power oppose the establishment of any one denomination in America," several Philadelphians wrote in 1768. "Religious establishments are very hardly kept from great corruption." When the Virginia House of Delegates sought to provide "for the legal support of Teachers of the Christian Religion," James Madison wrote his famous "Memorial and Remonstrance" to argue against any such state support for religion. "Who does not see that the same authority which can establish Christianity, in exclusion of all other religions, may establish with the same ease any particular sect of Christians, in exclusion of all other sects?" Madison asked. Like Williams before him, Madison worried that "the majority may trespass on the rights of the minority."[4]

Thomas Jefferson counted Virginia's "Act for Establishing Religious Freedom" among his greatest achievements. "The opinions of men are not the object of civil government, nor under its jurisdiction," Jefferson wrote, "and to restrain the profession or propagation of principles on supposition of their ill tendency is a dangerous falacy, which at once destroys all religious liberty."

Jefferson was confident that "truth is great and will prevail if left to herself."[5]

It's not that the founders were antireligious. Far from it. Although the views of Jefferson and a few others tended decidedly toward Deism, several of the founders held religious convictions that we would recognize today as Christian orthodoxy. But as observers of endless squabbles over religion in the Old World, some of which had carried over to the colonies, the founders thought the best posture for the fledgling nation would be for the government to stay out of the religion business, and thus was born this grand and unprecedented experiment of the First Amendment, which both proscribed the establishment of religion and ensured the free exercise of religion. In so doing the founders called upon the ideas of Roger Williams as well as the model of several of the Middle Colonies, including New York, New Jersey, and Pennsylvania, all of which had demonstrated that the way to accommodate religious pluralism was to shy away from religious establishment.[6]

The success of Rhode Island's experiment in church-state separation and religious liberty figured explicitly into the congressional debates surrounding the proposed Bill of Rights in 1789, discussions that produced the First Amendment. The line from Williams to the U.S. Constitution, then, is unbroken.[7]

Not every religious leader thought that disestablishment was a good idea. Lyman Beecher, Congregationalist minister in Litchfield, Connecticut, fought frantically against a plan to disestablish Congregationalism in Connecticut, fearing that religion would lose its influence in society. In 1820, however, within two years of disestablishment, Beecher was forced to repent. "Revivals now began to pervade the state," he wrote in his autobiography. "It cut the churches loose from dependence on state support. It threw them wholly on their own resources and on God." Beecher pronounced the separation of church and state "the best thing that ever happened to the State of Connecticut."[8]

As Beecher himself came to see, the effect of this radical idea of disestablishment has been electrifying. Various religious groups or entrepreneurs (to extend the free-market metaphor) have competed with one another throughout American history, thereby lending an energy and a dynamism to America's religious marketplace unparalleled in Western culture. The percentage of Americans who believe in God or a Supreme Being far outstrips that of other nations. In Great Britain, the established Church of England draws fewer than 800,000 of the population to its doors on any given Sunday, and leaders of the state Lutheran church in Sweden recently petitioned Parliament to be disestablished so that the church could enjoy the benefits of competing in the free marketplace of religion.

Given the resounding success of separating church and state, one would think that Baptists would be proud of their tradition's contribution to American society and to the vitality of religious life. Not so. Many leaders of the Religious Right, a good number of whom claim to be Baptists, would like nothing better than to dismantle the First Amendment by mandating public prayers in public schools, propagating taxpayer-funded school vouchers, and by posting religious documents, such as the Ten Commandments, in public places.[9]

On January 1, 1802, Jefferson responded to a letter from members of the Danbury Baptist Association, which had expressed concerns about a rumor that a particular religious group would be designated as the national church. Jefferson, seeking to allay their fears, penned his classic and oft-quoted response. "I contemplate with solemn reverence," the president wrote, "that act of the whole American people which declared that their legislature should 'make no law respecting the establishment of religion, of prohibiting the free exercise thereof,' thus building a wall of separation between church and State."[10]

Jefferson's letter to the Danbury Baptists in Connecticut has caused the Religious Right all manner of consternation in their attempts to subvert the disestablishment clause of the First Amendment. The first and most common rejoinder is to point out that the phrase "separation of church and state" is not language found explicitly in the Constitution. True enough; it *does* come from Jefferson, who was paraphrasing Roger Williams. But in order for that argument to have any traction, you would have to demonstrate that the phrase "separation of church and state" is not an accurate summation of the First Amendment itself, which reads: "Congress shall make no law respecting the establishment of religion, or prohibiting the free exercise thereof." When this argument fails, as inevitably it must, then the Religious Right relies on bluster. To cite one example, Rick Scarborough asserts, without elaboration, that those who support the separation of church and state "have resorted to extracting nine words from a private correspondence to validate their views, which is [*sic*] foreign to the Constitution's original intent." They take Jefferson's words "out of context," though the author doesn't demonstrate how they are acontextual.[11]

In one sense it is understandable that the Religious Right would want to distance itself from Williams, who articulated some harsh judgments about the dangers of church-state collusion. Principally, Williams was concerned that, in entangling church and state, political figures would be in a position to adjudicate the merits of various religious expressions. In a warning that anticipated the actions of the Religious Right, Williams feared that "the civil magistrate must reform the church, establish religion, and so consequently must first judge and judicially determine which is true [and] which is false." Williams worried, finally, that state sponsorship of religion would yield an unhappy situation wherein "the whole world must rule and govern the Church."[12]

And what if even the truest of true religions were established by the state? Williams doubted that such a designation would have an effect. In fact, the consequence was likely to be the reverse. It is, Williams observed, "opposite to the souls of all men who by persecutions are ravished into a dissembled worship which their hearts embrace not." State-favored religion, moreover, was pointless, especially in the context of religious pluralism wrought by the Protestant Reformation. Reflecting on the futility of the government dictating belief, Williams asked, "Where find you evidence of a whole nation, country or kingdom converted to the faith, and of Christ's appointing of a whole nation or kingdom to walk in one way of religion?"[13]

Williams also cherished the notion of "soul liberty," which, ostensibly at least, is one of the cornerstones of Baptist beliefs. Soul liberty protected individual conscience from the tyranny of the majority, a principle that Baptists, at least until recently, have always defended—in part because Baptists themselves began as a minority.

Isaac Backus, a Baptist who had separated from the Congregational established church in eighteenth-century New England, echoed Williams' dim view of government interventions in religion, or vice versa. Backus noted that Jesus himself "made no use of secular force in the first setting up of the Gospel-Church," even though he arguably could have used such help. "All acts of executive power in the civil state are to be performed in the name of the king or state they belong to," Backus wrote in his *Appeal to the Public for Religious Liberty* in 1773, "while all our religious acts are to be done in the *name of the Lord Jesus Christ* and so are to be performed *heartily as to the Lord and not unto men.*" Can government enforce fidelity to the faith? Backus thought not: "it is but *lip service* and *vain worship* if our *fear toward [God] is taught by the precepts of men.*"[14]

Those who would abrogate the First Amendment separation of church and state fail to comprehend both the teachings of Jesus and the lessons of history. As Backus noted, Jesus did not have the benefit of the state in the formation of his church, yet it flourished, extending beyond Palestine to the far corners of the world. The umbrella of state sanction beginning with the conversion of Constantine in 312 C.E. turned out, at best, to be a mixed blessing. An era known as the Dark Ages ensued, and by the sixteenth century, the church had become so corrupted by power that Martin Luther unleashed his Protestant Reformation to renew the church.

Another voice articulating Baptist principles on church-state separation rang out from the steps of the U.S. Capitol on May 16, 1920. On that Sunday afternoon, George Washington Truett, pastor of First Baptist Church in Dallas, Texas, walked to the lectern set up for him on the east steps of the Capitol in Washington, D.C. Truett opened with a paean to the United States and declared that "the supreme contribution of the new world to the old is the contribution of religious liberty." Indeed, it was "the chiefest contribution that America has thus far made to civilization," and Truett was proud to announce to his audience of fifteen thousand that the separation of church and state was "pre-eminently a Baptist achievement."[15]

Truett continued with a ringing endorsement of Baptist principles, especially civil and religious liberty. Baptists affirmed, he said, "the natural and fundamental and indefeasible right of every human being to worship God or not, according to the dictates of his conscience, and, as long as he does not infringe upon the rights of others, he is to be held accountable alone to God for all religious beliefs and practices." This principle extends beyond mere toleration to absolute liberty: "Toleration is a concession, while liberty is a right."

Like Backus before him, Truett interpreted the era after Constantine as disastrous for the church. "When Christianity first found its way into the city of the Ceasars it lived at first in cellars and alleys," he said, "but when Constantine crowned the union of church and state, the church was stamped with the spirit of the Caesars." Religion, Truett insisted, should be voluntary. "It is the consistent and insistent contention of our Baptist people, always and everywhere, that religion must be forever voluntary and uncoerced, and that it is not the prerogative of any power, whether civil or ecclesiastical, to compel men to conform to any religious creed or form of worship," he thundered. "God wants free worshipers and no other kind."

According to Truett, Baptists recognized that enjoying religious liberty for themselves entailed defending it for others. "A Baptist would rise at midnight to plead for absolute religious liberty," he declared, "for his Catholic neighbor, and for his Jewish neighbor, and for everybody else." And in a final salvo that might have anticipated the chicanery of Roy Moore seven decades later, Truett declared, "Christ's religion needs no prop of any kind from any worldly source, and to the degree that it is thus supported is a millstone hanged about its neck."

The subject of millstones brings us to another caper associated with the Religious Right, the installation of a granite monument emblazoned with the Ten Commandments in the lobby of the Judicial Building in Montgomery, Alabama. The instigator behind what became known as "Roy's Rock" was Roy S. Moore, formerly the chief justice of the Supreme Court of the state of Alabama, better known as the "Ten Commandments Judge."

Roy Stewart Moore attended the U.S. Military Academy at West Point, where he graduated in 1969. After military service as a military policeman in Vietnam—where he was known, not affectionately, as "Captain America" for his zeal—Moore returned to Alabama and earned his law degree in 1977 from the University of Alabama. After a stint as a deputy district attorney in Etowah County, he ran for a circuit court judgeship and was defeated badly. He headed then for Texas to embark on a career as a professional kickboxer and then to the outback of Australia. He returned to Alabama in 1984 and briefly set up private practice in Gadsden. Moore was then appointed to fill a vacant circuit court judgeship in Gadsden; he ran and won election to the bench in his own right in 1992. Moore opened his court sessions with prayer and hung a hand-carved wooden plaque depicting the Ten Commandments in his courtroom, an action that, his critics said, represented an infringement of the disestablishment clause of the First Amendment. The American Civil Liberties Union (ACLU) filed suit in 1995 to have the plaque removed. The people of Alabama, however, rather than censure his flouting of the Constitution, rewarded Moore by electing him chief justice of the Alabama Supreme Court in 2000; Moore, running as a Republican, had campaigned for office as the "Ten Commandments Judge."

Shortly after his election he commissioned a local gravestone company to produce a monument emblazoned with the Decalogue, financed by D. James Kennedy's Coral Ridge Ministries in Fort Lauderdale, Florida. Late in the evening of July 31, 2001, Moore and a work crew, laboring through the night, installed the two-and-one-half-ton granite monument, which would come to be known as Roy's Rock, in the lobby of the Alabama Judicial Building in Montgomery.

Because he had run for office as the Ten Commandments judge, Moore's action surprised no one. The ACLU had warned against it as an unconstitutional infringement of the establishment clause of the First Amendment. Other groups, religious and otherwise (including the Alabama Free Thought Association), had petitioned to have representations of *their* convictions posted in the Alabama Judicial Building, and, because of the proximity of the building to the Dexter Avenue Baptist Church just up the street, others suggested mounting a plaque with Martin Luther King Jr.'s "I Have a Dream" speech on the walls of the Judicial Building. Moore steadfastly refused all such entreaties. He wanted only the Decalogue.

As it had threatened, the ACLU brought action, joined in the case by Americans United for the Separation of Church and State and the Southern Poverty Law Center. Myron Thompson, U.S. district judge, heard arguments in October 2002 and rendered his verdict several months later: the installation of the monument, he ruled, especially because Moore refused to post other religious sentiments, represented a violation of the establishment clause of the First Amendment in that it clearly favored one tradition above all others and was therefore a religious statement and not, as Moore claimed, merely an acknowledgment of the roots of American jurisprudence. Thompson ordered the monument removed. Moore filed an appeal to the U.S. Court of Appeals and to the Supreme Court, but both refused to hear the case. He then vowed to defy the law. Judge Thompson was not amused. Moore's colleagues on the bench approved the removal of the monument, which was finally accomplished in August 2003. The Court of the Judiciary then heard arguments about the still-defiant chief justice and decided unanimously on November 13, 2003, to remove Moore from office for his flouting of federal law and for violating his oath to uphold the Constitution of the United States.[16]

The removal of Roy's Rock to a storage closet in the Alabama Judicial Building was a source of consternation to many of his followers, some of whom had frantically protested to the bitter end. For months since the Decalogue's installation, scores of buses had pulled up to the Judicial Building, disgorging the faithful, who would file into the lobby, drop to their knees, and pray in front of the granite monument. "Get your hands off my God!" one protester screamed when the court ordered its removal. Even beyond Alabama, the removal, in compliance with a federal court order, prompted all manner of wailing and gnashing of teeth on the part of conservatives, many of whom identified themselves as Baptists. This was a clear indication, they insisted, of the moral decline in American society. One hysterical screed circulated by e-mail predicted that the depiction of Moses and the Ten Commandments on the U.S. Supreme Court Building in Washington would soon disappear. A protester in Montgomery loudly declared that if you wanted to see the future of America—by which he meant, presumably, a future devoid of religious sentiment—consider the blank space in the lobby of the Judicial Building where Roy's Rock once sat.

Moore calls himself a Baptist, but Roy's Rock represents an utter repudiation of Baptist principles. Despite all the hysteria and overblown rhetoric surrounding its removal, the removal was proper, both to protect the state from sectarianism and to protect the faith from government sanction. "I do not believe it is for the interest of religion to invite the civil magistrate to direct its exercises, its discipline, or its doctrines," Jefferson wrote in 1808. The reason that the depiction of Moses and the Ten Commandments will not be chiseled from the U.S. Supreme Court Building anytime soon is that, unlike the case in Alabama, the frieze in Washington portrays one of several sources for American jurisprudence—and those sources are numerous, including the Code of Hammurabi, Confucius, the English Common Law tradition, and so on. Moore, on the other hand, sought to enshrine only one source (what he calls the "Judeo-Christian tradition"), and he steadfastly—even belligerently—refused to recognize any others. On that basis, Judge Thompson concluded that both the intent and the effect of the monument were to give the place of honor to one tradition, to the exclusion of all others. That, clearly, represents a violation of the First Amendment proscription against religious establishment.[17]

Moore styles himself an "originalist" in his approach to the Constitution, a term that is part of the coded language used by the Religious Right and by conservatives generally. An "originalist" or a "strict constructionist" holds that the Constitution is not a fluid and pliable document, that it should be interpreted according to the "original intent" of the framers. This notion, first popularized by Edwin Meese, Ronald Reagan's attorney general, and by Robert Bork, Reagan's nominee to the Supreme Court who was rejected by the Senate, insists on the narrowest possible reading of the Constitution. Most specifically, it has been invoked to counter the Supreme Court's *Roe v. Wade* decision of 1973, the ruling that guaranteed legal access to abortion by asserting that individual privacy was a constitutional right. Opponents of abortion seized on this, using the originalist language to argue that the framers of the Constitution never intended to guarantee individual privacy and, therefore, women have no such rights.[18]

Moore also invoked originalism in his crusade against the First Amendment, but to rather different ends. He asserted that when the founders talked about "free exercise of religion" they meant Christianity—or, in his more expansive moments, Moore extends the guarantee to what he calls the Judeo-Christian tradition. Because the framers had no experience of, say, Muslims or Hindus or Daoists, Moore argues—an assertion that is demonstrably false—their "original intent" was to secure for Americans the free exercise of Christianity alone. Under this originalist interpretation, in Moore's view, the First Amendment guarantees the free exercise of *Christianity* or the Judeo-Christian tradition. No other religious expression, according to Moore's originalist scheme, enjoys the protection of the U.S. Constitution. Relying on this doctrine of originalism, then, Moore can justify the posting of the Ten Commandments in public places while excluding all other religious representations, because the founders, he insists, were talking only about the Judeo-Christian tradition.

Originalism is compelling for its clarity and its simplicity; Antonin Scalia and Clarence Thomas frequently invoked it in their Supreme Court opinions. But the silliness of originalism becomes apparent when you try to apply it to the second clause of the First Amendment, the guarantee of a free press. Employing the same logic that Moore uses to justify the exclusion of religious expression other than Christianity—and, perhaps, Judaism—you would have to argue that freedom of the press extends strictly and exclusively to newspapers because newspapers were the only "press" that the framers knew at the end of the eighteenth century. A documentary filmmaker, then, or a television journalist, according to this narrow, originalist view, cannot claim a constitutional guarantee to freedom of the press because the framers did not have television in mind when they drafted the First Amendment.

For Moore and other conservatives, those who dissent from the originalist scheme, those who refuse to view the Constitution as a static document, are "judicial activists" and therefore represent a threat to America. Judicial activism, however, is in the eyes of the beholder. "There is a misconception that so-called activist judges who 'legislate from the bench' are invariably liberal," Adam Cohen of the *New York Times* noted. "In fact, conservative judges can be even more eager to overrule decisions made by elected officials." Cohen cited the reversals of environmental legislation and gun-control legislation by conservative jurists. A 2005 study by a professor at Yale Law School, moreover, demonstrated that the Supreme Court justice who had voted most often to overturn laws passed by Congress was Clarence Thomas, one of the heroes of the Religious Right for his putative conservativism, while the two justices least likely to be "judicial activists" were both Clinton appointees.[19]

Quite apart from all of the legal arguments concerning the First Amendment and the separation of church and state, and even beyond the overwhelming evidence that religious life has flourished in America as nowhere else precisely because of religious disestablishment, the even larger argument against conflating church and state is an argument that evangelicals know very well: the dangers of trivialization. Throughout American history evangelicals have been extraordinarily suspicious of formalism and empty ritual. When Theodorus Jacobus Frelinghuysen, a Dutch Pietist, arrived in New York City from the Netherlands in 1720, he castigated a fellow minister for using the Lord's Prayer in Dutch Reformed worship services, remarking that such ritual utterances were inimical to true piety. The holiness movement of the nineteenth century, to cite another of many examples, was a reaction against the perceived complacency of Methodism, which in turn had been an earlier effort to revitalize the Church of England. Holiness people gathered at camp meetings in places like Oak Bluffs, Massachusetts, and Ocean Grove, New Jersey, in an effort to reclaim a warmhearted, affective piety that had been compromised as Methodism became more status conscious and upwardly mobile. Evangelicals have always recognized the perils of institutionalization, or what Max Weber called "routinization." True religion, evangelicals have always believed, functions best outside of institutional constraints.

How peculiar, then, given this history, that evangelicals associated with the Religious Right would seek to enshrine Christianity as the faith of the nation through prescribed prayer in schools or government support for religious education, or by erecting religious monuments on government property, thereby projecting the appearance, if not the reality, of state sanction. Evangelicals, especially Baptists, know better. They have always opposed formalized prayer as empty ritual, what one eighteenth-century evangelical called the "old, rotten, and stinking routine of religion." Evangelicals throughout American history have preached against the dangers of trivializing the faith—and what could be more inimical to true piety than the recitation of prayers prescribed by the state or the fetishization of the Judeo-Christian tradition on a block of granite in a public building?[20]

The final irony behind the Religious Right's attempts to eviscerate the First Amendment is that evangelicals themselves, and Baptists

in particular, have been the primary beneficiaries of religious pluralism in America. They operated outside of the New England religious
establishment in the seventeenth and eighteenth centuries, and the
explosion of Baptist growth in the nineteenth century would have
been impossible—or at least considerably more difficult—without
the protections of the First Amendment, its proscription against religious establishment and its guarantee of free exercise.

From Williams to Backus to Truett and throughout American history, at least until recently, Baptists have been fierce guardians of
the First Amendment and the separation of church and state. Two
related developments in the late 1970s conspired to undermine that
noble tradition. First, the rise of the Religious Right—ironically
during the presidential administration of a Southern Baptist, Jimmy
Carter—and the conservative takeover of America's largest Protestant denomination, the Southern Baptist Convention, in 1979. The
effects of the former, organized by Paul Weyrich and Richard Viguerie and headed by Jerry Falwell, Tim La Haye, Ed McAteer, and others, were felt almost immediately. The Religious Right, according
to pollster Louis Harris, proved decisive in the presidential election
of 1980 and was a major force four years later. Ever since the 1980s,
religious conservatives have provided the Republican Party with its
most reliable constituency, much the way that labor unions once
formed the core of the Democratic Party.

In retrospect, it's not difficult to appreciate the motivations
behind the rise of the Religious Right. Ever since changes to the
immigration laws in 1965, the arrival of Asians and South Asians
has altered the religious landscape of the United States. Muslim
mosques, Hindu and Shintō temples, Buddhist stupas, and Sikh
gurdwārās now dot the countryside. By the late 1970s, the leaders
of the Religious Right felt their hegemony over American society
slipping away, and one reading of the Religious Right is that many
evangelicals felt that their faith could no longer compete in this
new, expanded religious marketplace. Rather than gear up for new

competition, the Religious Right, relying on their supposed ally in the White House, sought to change the rules to ensure their advantage in the 1980s.

The pursuit of power and influence in the 1980s, however, came at a price. For most of the twentieth century, evangelicalism had existed primarily within its own subculture, which nurtured individuals and kept them safe from the depredations of the world. It was an insular universe, and the most damning thing you could say about a fellow believer was that she or he was "worldly." The world outside of the subculture, including the political realm, was corrupt and corrupting, and believers had better beware.

Along about 1980, however, evangelicals, newly intoxicated with political power and cultural influence, began to let down their guard. They succumbed to the seductions of the culture. It was during the Reagan years when we began to hear about the so-called prosperity gospel, the notion that God will reward true believers with the emoluments of this world. Evangelicalism was still a subculture in the 1980s, but it was no longer a counterculture. It had lost its edge, its capacity for cultural critique, because it had become almost inseparable from the prevailing culture.

If the effects of the Religious Right were dramatic and easily discernible, the seizure of the Southern Baptists by conservatives, however, was more gradual, its effects evolutionary rather than revolutionary. In plotting their action in the late 1970s, Paul Pressler and Paige Patterson, architects of the takeover of the Southern Baptist Convention, recognized that the president of the convention had broad appointive powers over denominational agencies and even to the trustee boards of colleges and seminaries affiliated with the convention. Beginning with the election of Adrian Rogers in 1979, conservatives have elected other conservatives to the presidency in an unbroken line to the present. Each president has used his appointive powers to turn back what conservatives regard as the drift toward liberalism within the Southern Baptist Convention. But they didn't stop there. Lured by the prospect of political power during the Reagan years, the leaders of the Southern Baptist Convention steadily whittled away at their Baptist heritage. Instead of advocating the separation of church and state, they supported prescribed, compulsory prayer in public schools and, more recently, federal funding for faith-based initiatives and school vouchers for private education, including religious schools.

Roger Williams and Isaac Backus were representatives of religious minorities who looked to the government for protection from the entrenched, established majority. Their putative descendants, however, seek to impose their religious views on all Americans, thereby violating not only the First Amendment but the very principles that define their own religious heritage.

What leaders of the Religious Right fail to recognize, apparently, is the lesson that Lyman Beecher learned only belatedly: that religious disestablishment as mandated by the First Amendment is the best friend religion ever had. Put simply, religion has thrived in this country for more than two centuries precisely because the state has (for the most part, at least) stayed out of the religion business. The examples of other western nations suggest that once you begin to dictate religious belief or behavior—as with prescribed prayer in schools or Roy's Rock in Montgomery, Alabama—you kill it.

Even the Supreme Court has recognized this principle. "Religious beliefs worthy of respect," the Court declared in *Wallace v. Jaffree*, "are the product of free and voluntary choice by the faithful." So, too, "the individual's freedom to choose his own creed is the counterpart of his right to refrain from accepting the creed established by the majority."[21]

How peculiar that Roy Moore and many of his followers claim to be Baptists! I want to know why every Baptist in the state of Alabama didn't storm the Judicial Building after Moore installed his monument and demand that it be removed immediately, not merely because the monument itself became the subject of a kind of perverse idolatry—I wonder if Moore's followers remember the golden calf?—but, more basically, because it violated bedrock Baptist principles of soul liberty and freedom of individual conscience. Shame on every Baptist in Alabama who sat by silently and put up with this travesty.

Quite properly, Roy's Rock was removed from the lobby of Alabama's Judicial Building. The First Amendment prevailed over religious sectarianism and political chicanery. Still, I do think it's a shame that this imposing block of granite, the size and girth of a washing machine, was consigned to a storage room. The appropriate place for such a monument might be in one of Montgomery's many churches or even in Moore's front yard, as an expression of his personal convictions. Let him deal with the neighbors and the zoning board rather than tampering with the Constitution and with the venerable tradition of church-state separation, one of the bedrock principles of the Baptist tradition, that has served this nation remarkably well for more than two centuries.

What happens next? Those of us who number ourselves in the community of faith must resist being blinded by the blandishments of the culture. The lesson of the Protestant Reformation, and perhaps of the New Testament itself, is the treachery of institutions and government sanctions as guarantors of truth. Indeed, one of the reasons for evangelical success throughout American history is the alacrity with which evangelicals have found creative ways to operate outside of institutional boundaries, be it the open-air preaching of George Whitefield in the eighteenth century, the circuit riders of the nineteenth, or the creative use of media by Aimee Semple McPherson, Charles Fuller, and Billy Graham in the twentieth. Conversely, perhaps the greatest weakness of mainline Protestantism is its misplaced faith in and allegiance to institutions.

Like Jesus, standing on the ramparts overlooking the city, evangelicals must somehow find the courage and the will to resist the devil's cajoling, the temptations of authority and splendor and power and arrogance and cultural influence, recognizing that religion flourishes best at the margins of society and not at the centers of power. A granite monument in Alabama trivializes the faith and turns the Decalogue into a fetish. Let's recall the words of one protester on the steps of the Alabama Judicial Building: "Get your hands off my God!" If I'm not mistaken, one of the commandments chiseled into that granite block warns against graven images. Roger Williams remarked in 1644 about "how impossible it is for a dead stone to have fellowship with the living God."[22]

I fear that Baptist principles regarding the separation of church and state have all but disappeared. What was once a proud and mighty—and defining—tradition of ensuring that government not interfere with religion and religion not meddle with government has withered beneath the onslaughts of misguided individuals who seek to impose their own views on the rest of society. The gospel is compromised, American Protestantism is imperiled, and the republic itself suffers from the massive disappearance of Baptists from the American landscape.

Never in my life did I think I would say this, but America needs more Baptists. Sure, there are plenty of people who call themselves Baptists, especially in the South. But are they *really* Baptists? I think not, because they betray bedrock Baptists principles regarding soul liberty and separation of church and state.

America needs more Baptists—*real* Baptists, not counterfeit Baptists, those who are Baptist in name only because they would like nothing better than to eviscerate the First Amendment. Christianity itself needs more Baptists, women and men willing to reconnect with the scandal of the gospel and not chase after the chimera of state sanction, women and men prepared to stand on conviction and articulate the faith in the midst of a pluralistic culture—not by imposing their principles on the remainder of society, but by following the example of Jesus and doing what Baptists have always done best: preaching the gospel from the margins and not lusting after temporal power and influence.

Roy's Rock was consigned to a darkened storeroom, out of the public eye. It was shoved aside, along with other graven images throughout history. The gospel, however, endures. And it survives not because it has been idolized in a block of granite or because politicians deign to give it their blessing. It survives for the same reason it flourished in first-century Palestine and throughout the centuries—because believers have borne witness to its transformative power. Some of the best of these—we call them Baptists—have stoutly resisted the temptation to impose their understanding of the faith on others through the coercive mechanisms of the state.

"Baptists have one consistent record concerning liberty throughout their long and eventful history," George Washington Truett declared from the steps of the Capitol in 1920. "They have never been a party to oppression of conscience."

May it again be so. May it always be so.

NOTES

PREFACE: DEFINING AMERICAN EVANGELICALISM

1 Patrick Allitt, *Religion in America Since 1945: A History* (New York: Columbia University Press, 2003). For selective literalism, see Randall Balmer, *Thy Kingdom Come: How the Religious Right Distorts the Faith and Threatens America* (New York: Basic, 2006), chap. 1.

2 The Great Commission appears in Mark 16:15.

3 It's probably worth noting that Graham's son Franklin did the opposite.

1: AN ALTOGETHER CONSERVATIVE SPIRIT

1 Alexis de Tocqueville, *Democracy in America*, ed. Henry Steele Commager, trans. Henry Reeve (New York: Oxford University Press, 1947), 200.

2 Robert Baird, *Religion in America*, abridged ed. (New York: Harper & Row, 1970), 120, 110; Philip Schaff, *America: A Sketch of Its Political, Social, and Religious Character*, ed. Perry Miller (1855; repr., Cambridge, Mass.: Belknap Press of Harvard University Press, 1961), 11, 73.

3 Sidney E. Mead, *The Lively Experiment: The Shaping of Christianity in America* (New York: Harper & Row, 1963); Winthrop S. Hudson, *The Great Tradition of the American Churches* (New York: Harper, 1953).

4 See William G. McLoughlin, *New England Dissent, 1630–1833: The Baptists and the Separation of Church and State*, 2 vols. (Cambridge, Mass.: Harvard University Press, 1971); idem, *Isaac Backus and the American Pietistic Tradition* (Boston: Little, Brown, 1967); John M. Mulder, "William Livingston:

Propagandist against Episcopacy," *Journal of Presbyterian History* 54, no. 1 (1976): 83–104.

5 Perry Miller, *Roger Williams: His Contribution to the American Tradition* (Indianapolis: Bobbs-Merrill, 1953), 98.

6 Quoted in Daniel L. Dreisbach, "Thomas Jefferson, a Mammoth Cheese, and the 'Wall of Separation,'" in *Religion and the New Republic: Faith in the Founding of America*, ed. James H. Hutson (Lanham, Md.: Rowman & Littlefield, 2000), 85. Scholars disagree about whether Jefferson was directly aware of Williams' "wall of separation" metaphor.

7 John F. Wilson and Donald L. Drakeman, eds., *Church and State in American History: Key Documents, Decisions, and Commentary from the Past Three Centuries*, 3rd ed. (Boulder, Colo.: Westview, 2003), 74.

8 Quoted in Mead, *Lively Experiment*, 59.

9 Regarding the influences on the founders, see Garry Wills, *Inventing America: Jefferson's Declaration of Independence* (Garden City, N.Y.: Doubleday, 1978); James Tanis, "From Provinces and Colonies to Federated States: The Dutch-American Example" (paper given at the Tenth Rensselaerswyck Seminar, Albany, N.Y., September 19, 1987).

10 Wilson and Drakeman, *Church and State*, 30. T. H. Breen and Stephen Foster have argued that religious principles contributed to the stability of Puritan New England from settlement to the revocation of the charter. See "The Puritans' Greatest Achievement: A Study of Social Cohesion in Seventeenth-Century Massachusetts," *Journal of American History* 60, no. 1 (1973): 5–22; from July 8, 1663, charter, granted by Charles II, in Wilson and Drakeman, *Church and State*, 16.

11 The most votes that a Communist Party candidate for president has received was just over 100,000 (out of more than 38 million) in the election of 1932; the Communist presidential candidate received 36,386 votes in 1984 (Marvine Howe, "U.S. Communists May Not Field a 1988 Slate," *New York Times*, November 20, 1987).

12 On the Pew Survey, see "Religious Landscape Study," Pew Research Center, accessed December 1, 2015, http://www.pewforum.org/religious -landscape-study/; for the Center for Voting and Democracy, see "Voter Turnout," FairVote.org, accessed December 1, 2015, http://www.fairvote .org/research-and-analysis/voter-turnout/; Jose A. DelReal, "Voter Turnout in 2014 Was the Lowest Since WWII," *Washington Post*, November 10, 2014. Religion, of course, also serves as a conservative *social* force as well as political; for an excellent example of this, see Paul E. Johnson, *A Shopkeeper's Millennium: Society and Revivals in Rochester, New York, 1815–1837* (New York: Hill & Wang, 1978). See also Joseph R. Gusfield, *Symbolic Crusade: Status Politics and the American Temperance Movement* (Urbana: University of Illinois

Press, 1963); and Charles C. Cole Jr., *The Social Ideas of the Northern Evangelists, 1826–1860* (New York: Octagon, 1954).

13 *Washington's "Farewell Address" in Facsimile, with Transliterations of All the Drafts of Washington, Madison, & Hamilton, Together with their Correspondence and Other Supporting Documents*, ed. Victor Hugo Paltsits (New York: New York Public Library, 1935), 151. I express some hesitation about the Eisenhower quotation because there is no documented evidence that he actually said it, although it is frequently attributed to him; see Patrick Henry, " 'And I Don't Care What It Is': The Tradition-History of a Civil-Religion Proof Text," *Journal of the American Academy of Religion* 49, no. 1 (1981): 35–49; de Tocqueville, *Democracy in America*, 200.

14 Breen and Foster argue that the general prosperity of seventeenth-century New England contributed to its stability ("Puritans' Greatest Achievement").

15 Schaff, *America*, 12.

16 Schaff, *America*, 11, 79; Edward T. Corwin, ed., *Ecclesiastical Records: State of New York*, 7 vols. (Albany, N.Y.: State Historian, 1901–1916), 5:3460.

17 Schaff, *America*, 78; de Tocqueville, *Democracy in America,* 202.

18 "Religion in America: 50 Years: 1935–1985," *Gallup Report*, no. 236 (1985), 18, 50; "Religion in America," *Gallup Report*, no. 222 (1984), 28; Richard John Neuhaus, ed., *Unsecular America* (Grand Rapids: Eerdmans, 1986), 119; "Importance of Religion in One's Life," Pew Research Center, accessed December 1, 2015, http://www.pewforum.org/religious-landscape-study/importance-of-religion-in-ones-life/.

19 Quoted in Richard W. Pointer, *Protestant Pluralism and the New York Experience: A Study of Eighteenth-Century Religious Diversity* (Bloomington: Indiana University Press, 1988), 88; in Wilson and Drakeman, *Church and State*, 87.

20 Philip Norman, *Shout! The Beatles in Their Generation* (London: Mjf Books, 1981), 265–66; Francis X. Clines, "With Bare Churches, It's Barely England's Church," *New York Times,* May 11, 1987; Steve Doughty, "Just 800,000 Worshippers Attend a Church of England Service on the Average Sunday," *Daily Mail*, March 21, 2014.

21 On American latitudinarianism in religion, see Patricia U. Bonomi, *Under the Cope of Heaven: Religion, Society, and Politics in Colonial America* (New York: Oxford University Press, 1986), 218–20; Robert N. Bellah et al., *Habits of the Heart: Individualism and Commitment in American Life* (Berkeley: University of California Press, 1985), chap. 9.

22 Quoted in Edwin S. Gaustad, *Liberty of Conscience: Roger Williams in America* (Grand Rapids: Eerdmans, 1991), 167.

23 Quoted in Gaustad, *Liberty of Conscience*, 189.

2: TURNING WEST

1 Quoted in Larry Martin, ed., *The Topeka Outpouring of 1901* (Joplin, Mo.: Christian Life Books, 2000), 85.

2 Donald E. Miller, *Reinventing American Protestantism: Christianity in the New Millennium* (Berkeley: University of California Press, 1997); Kimon Howland Sargeant, *Seeker Churches: Promoting Traditional Religion in a Nontraditional Way* (New Brunswick, N.J.: Rutgers University Press, 2000); George M. Marsden, *The Soul of the American University: From Protestant Establishment to Established Nonbelief* (New York: Oxford University Press, 1994).

3 My meeting with Shuttlesworth took place in the spring of 2004.

3: CASTING ASIDE THE BALLAST OF HISTORY AND TRADITION

1 On the Second Awakening in New England, see David W. Kling, *A Field of Divine Wonders: The New Divinity and Village Revivals in Northwestern Connecticut, 1792–1822* (University Park: Pennsylvania State University Press, 1993); and Randolph A. Roth, *The Democratic Dilemma: Religion, Reform and the Social Order in the Connecticut River Valley of Vermont, 1791–1850* (Cambridge: Cambridge University Press, 1987). For an excellent biography of Dwight, see John R. Fitzmier, *New England's Moral Legislator: Timothy Dwight, 1752–1817* (Bloomington: Indiana University Press, 1998).

2 Some of the secondary sources on the Great Revival include John B. Boles, *The Great Revival, 1787–1805: The Origins of the Southern Evangelical Mind* (Lexington: University Press of Kentucky, 1972); and Christine Leigh Heyrman, *Southern Cross: The Origins of the Bible Belt* (New York: Knopf, 1997).

3 Paul K. Conkin, *Cane Ridge: America's Pentecost* (Madison: University of Wisconsin Press, 1990). On the Scottish origins of the camp-meeting tradition, see Leigh Eric Schmidt, *Holy Fairs: Scottish Communions and American Revivals in the Early Modern Period* (Princeton, N.J.: Princeton University Press, 1989).

4 Dickson D. Bruce Jr., *And They All Sang Hallelujah: Plain-Folk Camp-Meeting Religion, 1800–1845* (Knoxville: University of Tennessee Press, 1974).

5 B. W. Gorham, *Camp Meeting Manual, a Practical Book for the Camp Ground* (Boston: H. V. Degen, 1854); John F. Schermerhorn and Samuel J. Mills, *A Correct View of That Part of the United States Which Lies West of the Allegheny Mountains, with Regard to Religion and Morals* (Hartford: Peter B. Gleason, 1814), 41.

6 Quoted in Charles G. Finney, *Autobiography of Charles G. Finney* (New York: A. S. Barnes, 1876), 301; quoted in Charles C. Cole Jr., *The Social Ideas of the Northern Evangelists, 1826–1860* (New York: Octagon, 1954), 16; Whitney R. Cross, *The Burned-Over District: The Social and Intellectual History of Enthusiastic Religion in Western New York, 1800–1850* (New York: Harper &

Row, 1965); Paul E. Johnson, *A Shopkeeper's Millennium: Society and Revivals in Rochester, New York, 1815–1837* (New York: Hill & Wang, 1978); Curtis D. Johnson, *Islands of Holiness: Rural Religion in Upstate New York, 1790–1860* (Ithaca, N.Y.: Cornell University Press, 1989); quoted in Finney, *Autobiography of Charles G. Finney*, 301.

7 Quoted in Darrett B. Rutman, ed., *The Great Awakening: Event and Exegesis* (New York: Wiley, 1970), 157; quoted in William G. McLoughlin, ed., *The American Evangelicals, 1800–1900: An Anthology* (New York: Harper & Row, 1968), 87, 90.

8 Quoted in Nathan O. Hatch, *The Democratization of American Christianity* (New Haven, Conn.: Yale University Press, 1989), 139.

9 See Cole, *Social Ideas of the Northern Evangelists*; quoted in Hatch, *Democratization of American Christianity*, 62.

10 Quoted in Sydney E. Ahlstrom, *A Religious History of the American People* (New Haven, Conn.: Yale University Press, 1972), 491.

11 On the origins of premillennialism, see Ernest R. Sandeen, *The Roots of Fundamentalism: British and American Millenarianism, 1800–1930* (Chicago: University of Chicago Press, 1970).

12 Richard T. Hughes and C. Leonard Allen, *Illusions of Innocence: Protestant Primitivism in America, 1630–1875* (Chicago: University of Chicago Press, 1988).

13 Gal 3:28 (NIV).

14 For an excellent attempt to understand the political and ideological dimensions of this contradiction, see Edmund S. Morgan, *American Slavery, American Freedom: The Ordeal of Colonial Virginia* (New York: Norton, 1975).

4: AN END TO UNJUST INEQUALITY IN THE WORLD

1 James E. Pilcher, *Life and Labors of Elijah H. Pilcher of Michigan: Fifty-Nine Years a Minister of the Methodist Episcopal Church* (New York: Hunt & Eaton, 1892), 106, 118, 89, 116–17.

2 Pilcher, *Life and Labors*, 115–16.

3 S. H. Waldo, "The Evidence of the World's Ultimate Reform," *Oberlin Quarterly Review* 4 (1849): 288. Emphasis in original.

4 Quoted in George P. Fisher, *Life of Benjamin Silliman, M.D., LL.D.*, 2 vols. (New York: Charles Scribner, 1866), 1:83; Samuel Merwin and Nathaniel William Taylor, "Revival in New-Haven," *Christian Spectator* 3, no. 1 (1821): 49–52; "Revival of Religion in Yale College," *Connecticut Evangelical Magazine and Religious Intelligencer* 8, no. 5 (1815): 192; "Revival in Yale College," *Mutual Rights and Methodist Protestant*, May 20, 1831, 157. See also "Yale College," *Religious Intelligencer*, April 7, 1821, 736.

5 "Glorious Intelligence from Vermont," *Christian Intelligencer*, September 21, 1821, 26; "Revival in Castine, Me.," *Essex North Register*, March 18, 1836, 2; "Extract from an Article, Entitled, 'General View of Revivals in Vermont,'" *Christian Intelligencer*, September 21, 1821, 80; "Revivals of Religion," *Missionary Herald* 17, no. 3 (1821): 94; "Review of Evangelical Feeling," *Latter Day Luminary*, August 1, 1821, 442.

6 "Revivals in New-York State," *Hopkinsian Magazine*, March 1, 1825, 359; "Revivals in New York," *Pittsburgh Recorder*, October 11, 1825, 350; "Revivals in the Western Part of New-York," *Home Missionary*, October 1, 1831, 108.

7 Charles Grandison Finney, *Memoirs of Rev. Charles G. Finney, Written by Himself* (New York: A. S. Barnes, 1876), 24. On Finney, see also Keith J. Hardman, *Charles Grandison Finney, 1792–1875: Revivalist and Reformer* (Syracuse, N.Y.: Syracuse University Press, 1987); and Charles E. Hambrick-Stowe, *Charles G. Finney and the Spirit of American Evangelicalism* (Grand Rapids: Eerdmans, 1996).

8 "Revival in Rochester, N.Y.," *Christian Advocate & Journal*, April 28, 1827, 134; "Revival at Rochester," *Baptist Chronicle*, December 1, 1830, 190; "Religious Revivals," *Rhode Island Journal*, May 27, 1831, 42; "Revival at Rochester, N.Y." *Morning Star*, June 13, 1833, 27; "Revivals among the Africans in Rochester," *African Repository & Colonial Journal*, April 1, 1831, 61.

9 Finney, *Sermons on Gospel Themes* (Oberlin, Ohio: E. J. Goodrich, 1876), 348, 356.

10 "Jesus Christ a Moral and Religious Reformer," *Christian Reformer; or, Evangelical Miscellany*, July 1, 1828, 2ff.

11 Finney, "The Pernicious Attitude of the Church on the Reforms of the Age," in Donald Dayton, *Discovering an Evangelical Heritage* (1976; repr., Peabody, Mass.: Hendrickson, 1988), 21; "Means of Reform," *Religious Monitor & Evangelical Repository* 14 (1837): 281. Emphasis in original. Dayton's book (together with many of his other writings) makes a compelling case for the importance and range of progressive evangelicalism in the nineteenth century.

12 "On Mercy," *Piscataqua Evangelical Magazine* 2, no. 5 (1806): 181; "Faith and Works Inseparable," *Christian Examiner and Theological Review* 5 (1828): 545; "National Feeling," *Christian Spectator* 7, no. 11 (1825): 582.

13 W. J. Rorabaugh, *The Alcoholic Republic: An American Tradition* (New York: Oxford University Press, 1979).

14 "Thoughts on the Importance and Improvement of Common Schools," *Christian Spectator*, n.s. 1 (1827): 85.

15 Hugh Davis, *Joshua Leavitt: Evangelical Abolitionist* (Baton Rouge: Louisiana State University Press, 1990), 40; "Means Enjoyed by This Country for Promoting the Highest Interests," *Quarterly Christian Spectator* 6, no. 1 (1834): 36.

16 "On Sabbath Schools," *Christian Spectator* 1 (1829): 350, 246–347; "Importance of Sabbath Schools," *Christian Chronicle*, June 13, 1818, 141. See also Anne M. Boylan, *Sunday School: The Formation of an American Tradition, 1790–1880* (New Haven, Conn.: Yale University Press, 1988).

17 "On Sabbath Schools—Letter II," *Christian Spectator* 1, no. 8 (1819): 403; "Missionary Efforts for Education," *Literary and Evangelical Magazine* 9, no. 12 (1826): 663; Charles Dillingham, "Education of the Deaf and Dumb," *Literary and Evangelical Magazine* 11, no. 11 (1828): 587. On the coercive, even violent nature of Indian schools, see David Wallace Adams, *Education for Extinction: American Indians and the Boarding School Experience, 1875–1928* (Lawrence: University Press of Kansas, 1995).

18 "Necessity of a Better System of Instruction," *Virginia Evangelical & Literary Magazine* 1, no. 6 (1818): 255, 260, 259; "Amherst Charity College," *Evangelical Monitor*, September 8, 1821, 84. Emphasis in original.

19 "The Poor—the Half Not Told," *Western Christian Advocate*, December 25, 1835, 138; Ebenezer Elliot, "Wrong Not the Laboring Poor," *Evangelical Magazine and Gospel Advocate*, September 3, 1841, 288; "Blessed Is He That Considereth the Poor," *Western Christian Advocate*, June 13, 1834, 27. Emphasis in original.

20 "Prison Discipline Society," *Zion's Herald*, June 7, 1826, 4, 23; "Dying Confession of Joseph Hare, Remarks on the Penitentiary, &c," *Virginia Evangelical & Literary Magazine* 1, no. 12 (1818): 553, 554–55.

21 James H. Fairchild, "Woman's Rights and Duties," *Oberlin Quarterly Review* 4 (1849): 236–37, 346. The pagination in this fascicle appears to be haphazard.

22 C. C. Foote, "Woman's Rights and Duties," *Oberlin Quarterly Review* 4 (1849): 383, 406–7, 396. Emphasis in original.

23 "Women Not Unequal to Men," *Literary and Evangelical Magazine* 11, no. 8 (1828): 434; "The Mental Capacities of the Sexes Considered," *Evangelical Magazine and Gospel Advocate*, October 1, 1841, 315. Emphasis in original.

24 "Address," *Zion's Herald*, January 9, 1823, 1.

25 "Liberty, No. 11," *Herald of Gospel Liberty*, January 19, 1809, 41; "Liberty, No. 31," *Herald of Gospel Liberty*, February 2, 1810, 149; "Singular," *Herald of Gospel Liberty*, November 10, 1809, 126; "Liberty, No. 33," *Herald of Gospel Liberty*, March 2, 1810, 157.

26 "Liberty, No. 54," *Herald of Gospel Liberty*, April 15, 1814, 585–86. Emphasis in original.

27 Josiah Bushnell Grinnell, *Men and Events of Forty Years: Autobiographical Rem-iniscences of an Active Career from 1850 to 1890* (Boston: D. Lothrop, 1801), 11, 49; "Josiah Bushnell Grinnell," *Columbia Encyclopedia*, 6th ed. (New York: Columbia University Press, 2008).

28 L. F. Parker, "Josiah Bushnell Grinnell," *Annals of Iowa*, 3rd ser., 2 (1896): 249–59; Grinnell, *Men and Events of Forty Years*, 87, 88, 115.

29 On nativism, see Grinnell, *Men and Events of Forty Years*, 105–6; on women's rights, see p. 116.

30 Finney, *Sermons on Gospel Themes*, 352, 354. Finney upheld Bible societies as business models. On Roman Catholic attitudes toward affluence and, especially, private property, see E. Brooks Holifield, *Theology in America: Christian Thought from the Age of the Puritans to the Civil War* (New Haven, Conn.: Yale University Press, 2003), 418.

31 "Mr. Finney's Lectures on Christian Duty," *New-York Evangelist*, February 13, 1836, 26.

32 "The Moral Influence of 'Money-Making,' " *New-York Evangelist*, March 12, 1836, 41.

33 "The Farmer in Hard Times," *New-York Evangelist*, July 22, 1837, 118; "Stew-ardship of Wealth," *New-York Evangelist*, January 2, 1836, 1; "Reflections on Wealth," *Christian Chronicle*, November 7, 1818, 314.

34 "Necessity of a Better System of Instruction," 258; "Means Enjoyed by This Country for Promoting the Highest Interests," 47. Emphasis in original.

35 "On Usury," *Virginia Evangelical & Literary Magazine* 2, no. 2 (1819): 70; "On Some Probably Moral Effects of the Present Scarcity of Money," *Virginia Evangelical & Literary Magazine* 3, no. 2 (1820): 75. Emphasis in original.

36 "The Practice of Bearing Arms," *Western Christian Advocate*, March 13, 1835, 184; "The Late Duel," *Zion's Herald*, March 14, 1838, 43. Emphasis in origi-nal; "Duelling Law," *Zion's Herald*, April 18, 1838, 9, 16.

37 "New-York Peace Society," *Christian Spectator* 1, no. 4 (1819): 210; "From the Vermont Journal," *Christian Chronicle*, December 19, 1818, 391ff.

38 Merle E. Curti, "Non-Resistance in New England," *New England Quarterly* 2, no. 1 (1929): 36.

39 Curti, "Non-Resistance in New England," 35, 45, 47.

40 "Peace," *New-York Evangelist*, April 1, 1837, 53; "Peace," *New-York Evangelist*, April 22, 1837, 65.

41 Thomas C. Upham, "Essay on a Congress of Nations," in *Prize Essays on a Con-gress of Nations, for the Adjustment of International Disputes and for the Promotion of Universal Peace without Resort to Arms*, ed. William Ladd (Boston: American Peace Society, 1840), 356, 387, 373.

42 Upham, "Essay on a Congress of Nations," 373–74.

43 "The Cause of Peace," *New-York Evangelist*, December 16, 1837, 201.

44 Wm. B. Brown, "Religious Organizations and Slavery," *Oberlin Quarterly Review* 4 (1849): 415.

45 Charles Finney, *Lectures to Professing Christians Delivered in the City of New York, in the Years 1836 and 1837* (New York: J. S. Taylor, 1837), 321; "Rev. C. W. Gardner's Sermon," *New-York Evangelist*, June 24, 1837, 102.

46 "Thoughts on Slavery," *Virginia Evangelical & Literary Magazine* 2, no. 7 (1819): 293, 294, 295; "Negro Slavery," *Evangelical Witness* 2, no. 9 (1824): 410.

47 Upham, "Essay on a Congress of Nations," 383–84.

48 "Mr. Finney's Lectures on Christian Duty," 26.

49 Edward J. Blum, *Reforging the White Republic: Race, Religion, and American Nationalism, 1865–1898* (Baton Rouge: Louisiana State University Press, 2005), 181, 176, 178. Blum argues that Willard's overtures to Southern women were part of a larger process of unifying North and South along racially stratified lines.

50 *Official Proceedings of the Democratic National Convention Held in Chicago, Illinois, July 7, 8, 9, 10, and 11, 1896* (Chicago, 1896), 226–34, reprinted in *The Annals of America,* vol. 12, *1895–1904: Populism, Imperialism, and Reform* (Chicago: Encyclopaedia Britannica, 1968), 100–105; quoted in Michael Kazin, *A Godly Hero: The Life of William Jennings Bryan* (New York: Knopf, 2006), 121. Kazin's book is the definitive biography of Bryan.

51 Matthew Avery Sutton, *Aimee Semple McPherson and the Resurrection of Christian America* (Cambridge, Mass.: Harvard University Press, 2007), 214, 218, 219; Roberta Salter, interview with the author, New York City, September 27, 2001.

52 On evangelical activity in the 1930s and beyond, see Joel A. Carpenter, *Revive Us Again: The Reawakening of American Fundamentalism* (New York: Oxford University Press, 1997). On the precursors to the Religious Right, see Darren Dochuk, *From Bible Belt to Sun Belt: Plain-Folk Religion, Grassroots Politics, and the Rise of Evangelical Conservativism* (New York: Norton, 2011); and Daniel K. Williams, *God's Own Party: The Making of the Christian Right* (New York: Oxford University Press, 2010).

53 Quoted in Cal Thomas and Ed Dobson, *Blinded by Might: Can the Religious Right Save America?* (Grand Rapids: Zondervan, 1999), 206–9.

54 Quoted in Thomas and Dobson, *Blinded by Might*, 214.

55 Harold E. Hughes, *The Man from Ida Grove: A Senator's Personal Story* (Lincoln, Va.: Chosen Books, 1979), 230, 234. The Gospel reference is Matt 25:40.

56 The Pauline reference is Gal 3:28.

5: THY KINGDOM COME

1 Russell, founder of the Jehovah's Witnesses, insisted that a spiritual translation had indeed occurred in 1878. At that moment, those among the elect

who had died were raised into heaven, and thereafter anyone of the elect still living in 1878 would be translated immediately upon death into Christ's presence; they would not linger in the grave. See Alan Rogerson, *Millions Now Living Will Never Die: A Study of Jehovah's Witnesses* (London: Constable, 1969); Albert V. Vandenberg, "Charles Taze Russell: Pittsburgh Prophet, 1879–1909," *Western Pennsylvania Historical Magazine* 69 (1986): 3–20; and Edwin Scott Gaustad, *Dissent in American Religion* (Chicago: University of Chicago Press, 1973), 114–16. On the Good Friday vigil, see Barbara Grizzuti Harrison, *Visions of Glory: A History and a Memory of Jehovah's Witnesses* (New York: Simon & Schuster, 1978), 51; and Rogerson, *Millions Now Living*, 9.

2 *Signs of the Times*, April 15, 1840, 14. Much of Miller's biographical details are taken from Everett N. Dick, "The Millerite Movement, 1830–1845," in *Adventism in America: A History*, ed. Gary Land (Grand Rapids: Eerdmans, 1986), 9, 13–15.

3 Dick, "Millerite Movement," in Land, *Adventism in America*, 18.

4 Dick, "Millerite Movement," in Land, *Adventism in America*, 29–30; on the "ascension robes," see idem, 21–22. Regarding this rather tortuous transition, see Jonathan Butler, "From Millerism to Seventh-Day Adventism: 'Boundlessness to Consolidation,'" *Church History* 55 (1986): 50–64. On Seventh-Day Adventist membership statistics, see Land, *Adventism in America*, appendix 2.

5 See Pauline Moffitt Watts, "Prophecy and Discovery: On the Spiritual Origins of Christopher Columbus's 'Enterprise of the Indies,'" *American Historical Review* 90 (1985): 73–102. Watts argues that, although the historiography (especially Samuel Eliot Morison's *The Admiral of the Ocean Sea*) has portrayed Columbus as a man of science and rationality, Columbus was increasingly consumed by apocalyptic ideology and his own destiny.

6 Carl Whorley, who describes himself as pastor/teacher at the Tanglewood Baptist Church, Roanoke, Va., offers a fairly standard evangelical definition for rapture. He defines it as a "special event when the Lord Jesus Christ Himself will come down from heaven and hover over the earth. He will call the dead, born-again Christians out of the grave, and then after that the saints who are alive and still on this earth at this event. He will then take them off of the earth as well and take them back to heaven to be with Him" (transcription taken from cassette tape titled "The Rapture of the Church," distributed by Tanglewood Baptist Church).

7 For a survey of various views, see Robert G. Clouse, ed., *The Meaning of the Millennium: Four Views* (Downers Grove, Ill.: InterVarsity, 1977). Timothy P. Weber has diagramed some of the various possibilities; see *Living in the*

Shadow of the Second Coming: American Premillennialism 1875–1982, 2nd ed. (Grand Rapids: Zondervan, 1983), 10.

8 For Edwards' apocalyptic views, see *The Works of Jonathan Edwards*, ed. Stephen J. Stein, vol. 5, *Apocalyptic Writings* (New Haven, Conn.: Yale University Press, 1977), esp. 27–29; quoted in Robert S. Fogarty, ed., *American Utopianism* (Itasca, Ill.: F. E. Peacock, 1972), 18. For an explication of complex marriage and its millennial justification, see Constance Noyes Robertson, *Oneida Community: An Autobiography, 1851–1876* (Syracuse, N.Y.: Syracuse University Press, 1970), chap. 9. For an argument on the centrality of apocalyptic views for evangelicalism, see Matthew Avery Sutton, *American Apocalypse: A History of Modern Evangelicalism* (Cambridge, Mass.: Belknap Press of Harvard University Press, 2014).

9 Nathan O. Hatch, *The Sacred Cause of Liberty: Republican Thought and the Millennium in Revolutionary New England* (New Haven, Conn.: Yale University Press, 1977); Ruth Bloch, *Visionary Republic: Millennial Themes in American Thought, 1756–1800* (Cambridge: Cambridge University Press, 1985), chaps. 2–4; quoted in Peter N. Moore, "Westward the Course of Empire: Hermon Husband and the Frontier Millennium," typescript of a paper lent by the author. On the connection between New Light evangelicalism and patriotism, see also Alan Heimert, *Religion and the American Mind from the Great Awakening to the Revolution* (Cambridge, Mass.: Harvard University Press, 1966). Melvin B. Endy Jr. takes issue with interpretations of the American Revolution that posit strong undercurrents of millennialism in the Patriot rhetoric. Endy insists that evangelicals more often cast their rationalizations for Revolution in the language of just war theory. See "Just War, Holy War, and Millennialism in Revolutionary America," *William and Mary Quarterly*, 3rd ser., 42, no. 1 (1985): 3–25. On Husband, see also Bloch, *Visionary Republic*, 72–74, 113–14, 182–84.

10 This latter point is made by Douglas W. Frank, *Less Than Conquerors: How Evangelicals Entered the Twentieth Century* (Grand Rapids: Eerdmans, 1986), 67. Hatch touches on this as well in "Millennialism and Popular Religion in the Early Republic," in *The Evangelical Tradition in America*, ed. Leonard I. Sweet (Macon, Ga.: Mercer University Press, 1984), 113–30. On millennial themes in early American history, see James West Davidson, *The Logic of Millennial Thought: Eighteenth-Century New England* (New Haven, Conn.: Yale University Press, 1977); Hatch, *Sacred Cause of Liberty*; Bloch, *Visionary Republic*; James H. Moorhead, "Between Progress and Apocalypse: A Reassessment of Millennialism in American Religious Thought, 1800–1880," *Journal of American History* 71 (1984): 524–42; and Ernest Lee Tuveson, *Redeemer Nation: The Idea of America's Millennial Role* (Chicago: University of Chicago Press, 1968). Regarding the various social-reform movements

arising out of the Second Great Awakening, see Timothy L. Smith, *Revivalism and Social Reform in Mid-Nineteenth-Century America* (Nashville: Abingdon, 1967); Charles I. Foster, *An Errand of Mercy: The Evangelical United Front, 1790–1837* (Chapel Hill: University of North Carolina Press, 1960); and Anne M. Boylan, "Women in Groups: An Analysis of Women's Benevolent Organizations in New York and Boston, 1797–1840," *Journal of American History* 71 (1984): 497–523.

11 William G. McLoughlin says that the message of this song is "one of millennial faith and optimistic conviction that God has chosen the United States of America to lead the way to the redemption of the world for Christian freedom" (McLouglin, ed., *The American Evangelicals, 1800–1900: An Anthology* [New York: Harper & Row, 1968], 28; "The Battle Hymn of the Republic" is reproduced on pp. 28–29).

12 Quoted in James H. Moorhead, *American Apocalypse: Yankee Protestants and the Civil War, 1860–1869* (New Haven, Conn.: Yale University Press, 1978), ix. Moorhead's book is an excellent, extended study of the millennial views of northern Protestants during the Civil War.

13 William Robbins, "Mormons Go Back to a Sacred Valley in Missouri," *New York Times*, August 14, 1985. On Mormon millennialism, see Klaus Hansen, *Quest for Empire: The Political Kingdom of God and the Council of Fifty* (East Lansing: Michigan State University Press, 1967); and Grant Underwood, "Early Mormon Millenarianism: Another Look," *Church History* 54 (1985): 215–29.

14 Quoted in Eric Foner, ed., *Great Lives Observed: Nat Turner* (Englewood Cliffs, N.J.: Prentice-Hall, 1971), 45; quoted in Milton C. Sernett, ed., *Afro-American Religious History: A Documentary Witness* (Durham, N.C.: Duke University Press, 1985), 95. Emphasis in original.

15 On the eclipse of postmillennialism in the late nineteenth century, see Weber, *Living in the Shadow*, chap. 2; James H. Moorhead, "The Erosion of Postmillennialism in American Religious Thought, 1865–1925," *Church History* 53 (1984): 61–77. Moorhead argues that postmillennialism collapsed, in effect, beneath its own weight, that it could be sustained only in a culture dominated by evangelical values.

16 For a discussion of Darby's views and their implications, see Weber, *Living in the Shadow*, chap. 1. On the transition from postmillennialism to premillennialism and its importance to American evangelicals, see George M. Marsden, *Fundamentalism and American Culture: The Shaping of Twentieth-Century Evangelicalism, 1870–1925* (New York: Oxford University Press, 1980), 48–55; Moorhead, "Erosion of Postmillennialism"; and Frank, *Less Than Conquerors*, chap. 3. Frank sees the evangelical shift to premillennialism as an attempt to "recapture their control of history" (67). On the influence of

British millennial ideas in nineteenth-century America, see Ernest R. Sandeen, *The Roots of Fundamentalism: British and American Millenarianism, 1800–1930* (Chicago: University of Chicago Press, 1970).

17 Quoted in McLoughlin, *American Evangelicals, 1800–1900*, 184; Grant Wacker, "Marching to Zion: Religion in a Modern Utopian Community," *Church History* 54, no. 4 (1985): 496–511, esp. 505; quoted in Weber, *Living in the Shadow*, 88.

18 The *Scofield Reference Bible* remains popular. Oxford University Press, according to Cynthia Read, religion editor, has sold well over two million copies since 1967, 85 percent of them leather bound (an indication that the overwhelming majority of copies sold are for personal, devotional use, rather than for use in libraries).

19 Evangelicals see the creation of the state of Israel in 1948 as the fulfillment of the prophecy found in Jer 29:14: "I will be found by you, says the Lord, and I will restore your fortunes and gather you from all the nations and all the places where I have driven you, says the Lord, and I will bring you back to the place from which I sent you into exile" (RSV). Quoted in William Martin, "Waiting for the End: The Growing Interest in Apocalyptic Prophecy," *Atlantic Monthly*, June 1982, 35; cf. George Marsden, "Lord of the Interior," *Reformed Journal* 31 (1981): 2–3. See, for example, Lawrence Wright, "Letter from Jerusalem: Forcing the End," *New Yorker*, July 20, 1998, 42–53. The requirement for a red heifer derives from Num 19.

20 Evangelical hymns are replete with references to the coming millennium. Fanny Crosby's hymn, "Will Jesus Find Us Watching?" provides one example:

> When Jesus comes to reward His servants,
> Whether it be noon or night,
> Faithful to Him will He find us watching
> With our lamps all trimmed and bright?

> Blessed are those whom the Lord finds watching,
> In His glory they shall share;
> If He shall come at dawn or midnight,
> Will He find us watching there?

(Quoted in Weber, *Living in the Shadow*, 60.) Another, more recent song, written by Andraé Crouch, reads in part:

> It won't be long till we'll be leaving here.
> It won't be long. We'll be going home.

21 Martin, "Waiting for the End," 31. As in the nineteenth century, twentieth-century black visions of the apocalypse take a slightly different form. The

Honorable Elijah Muhammad taught that after six thousand years of white dominance, the "spook civilization" would come to an end about the year 2000. For the most compelling exposition of these ideas, see Malcolm X, *The Autobiography of Malcolm X* (New York: Grove, 1964), chaps. 10–11.

6: A PENTECOST OF POLITICS

1 Harry S. Stout, "Religion, Communications, and the Ideological Origins of the American Revolution," *William and Mary Quarterly* 3rd ser., 34, no. 4 (1977): 519–41; Alexis de Tocqueville, *Democracy in America*, ed. Richard D. Heffner (New York: New American Library, 1956), 91; Daniel Walker Howe, "Religion and Politics in the Antebellum North," in *Religion and American Politics: From the Colonial Period to the 1980s*, ed. Mark A. Noll (New York: Oxford University Press, 1990), 124–25. Emphasis in original.

2 See Rhys Isaac, *The Transformation of Virginia, 1740–1790* (Chapel Hill: Institute of Early American History and Culture, Williamsburg, Va., by University of North Carolina Press, 1982), 267–69; quoted in Robert W. Cherny, *A Righteous Cause: The Life of William Jennings Bryan* (Boston: Little, Brown, 1985), 58.

3 Peter Cartwright, *The Autobiography of Peter Cartwright* (Nashville: Abingdon, 1956), 43.

4 Quoted in Selwyn Rabb, "Taking on Tammany, 100 Years Ago," *New York Times*, February 14, 1992.

5 Quoted in William Martin, *A Prophet with Honor: The Billy Graham Story* (New York: W. Morrow, 1991), 111; Philip Schaff, *America: A Sketch of Its Political, Social, and Religious Character*, ed. Perry Miller (Cambridge, Mass.: Belknap Press of Harvard University Press, 1961), 95.

6 Quoted in James Tanis, *Dutch Calvinistic Pietism in the Middle Colonies: A Study in the Life and Theology of Theodorus Jacobus Frelinghuysen* (The Hague: Martinus Nijhoff, 1967), 54; quoted in Randall Balmer, *A Perfect Babel of Confusion: Dutch Religion and English Culture in the Middle Colonies* (New York: Oxford University Press, 1989), 127, 125.

7 Quoted in Leigh Eric Schmidt, "'A Second and Glorious Reformation': The New Light Extremism of Andrew Croswell," *William and Mary Quarterly*, 3rd ser., 43, no. 2 (1986): 222; Stout and Peter Onuf, "James Davenport and the Great Awakening in New London," *Journal of American History* 70, no. 3 (1983): 556–78. Emphasis in original.

8 Isaac, *Transformation of Virginia*, passim; Richard L. Bushman, ed., *The Great Awakening: Documents on the Revival of Religion, 1740–1745* (New York: Institute of Early American History and Culture at Williamsburg, Va., by Atheneum, 1970), 50, 57.

9 John F. Wilson and Donald Drakeman, eds., *Church and State in American History: The Burden of Religious Pluralism*, 2nd ed. (Boston: Beacon, 1987), 59.

10 Richard Allen, *The Life Experience and Gospel Labors of the Rt. Rev. Richard Allen* (Nashville: Abingdon, 1983), 30.

11 Quoted in Nathan O. Hatch, *The Democratization of American Christianity* (New Haven, Conn.: Yale University Press, 1989), 20.

12 Cartwright, *Autobiography of Peter Cartwright*, 61.

13 Betty I. Young, "A Missionary/Preacher as America Moved West: The Ministry of John Wesley Osborne," *Methodist History* 24 (1986): 195–215, esp. 207; *The American Colporteur System* (New York: American Tract Society, 1836), 3; reprinted in *The American Tract Society Documents, 1824–1925* (New York: Arno, 1972). Emphasis in original.

14 *American Colporteur System*, 7, 9. Emphasis in original.

15 Young, "Missionary/Preacher as America Moved West," 208–9.

16 *Instructions of the Executive Committee of the American Tract Society, to Colporteurs and Agents, with Statements of the History, Character, and Object of the Society* (New York: American Tract Society, 1868), 47; reprinted in American Tract Society Documents.

17 *Instructions of the Executive Committee of the American Tract Society*, 38–39.

18 Douglas Frank, *Less than Conquerors: How Evangelicals Entered the Twentieth Century* (Grand Rapids: Eerdmans, 1986), 173–79. See also Robert F. Martin, *Hero of the Heartland: Billy Sunday and the Transformation of American Society, 1862–1935* (Bloomington: Indiana University Press, 2002); and Lyle W. Dorsett, *Billy Sunday and the Redemption of Urban America* (Grand Rapids: Eerdmans, 1991).

19 See Matthew Avery Sutton, *Aimee Semple McPherson and the Resurrection of Christian America* (Cambridge, Mass.: Harvard University Press, 2007); Edith L. Blumhofer, *Aimee Semple McPherson: Everybody's Sister* (Grand Rapids: Eerdmans, 1993); and William G. McLoughlin, "Aimee Semple McPherson: 'Your Sister in the King's Glad Service,'" *Journal of Popular Culture* 1, no. 3 (1967): 193–217.

20 Quoted in Cherny, *Righteous Cause*, 60.

21 Quoted in Cherny, *Righteous Cause*, 34.

7: A LOFTIER POSITION

1 Robert J. Samuelson, "Great Expectations," *Newsweek*, January 8, 1996, 27.

2 Bailey Smith on *Larry King Live*, March 21, 1989.

3 Edward M. Brandt, "Mother," *The Way of Truth* 47 (1989): 2.

4 Barbara A. Peil, "A Seasoned Approach," *Kindred Spirit* 11 (1987): 13; "Motherhood in the '90s," *Focus on the Family* 14 (1990): 2; Brandt, "Mother," ii, 1.

5 Peil, "Seasoned Approach," 12.

6 Peil, "Seasoned Approach," 12, 13. This argument is made forcefully and compellingly by R. Marie Griffith in *God's Daughters: Evangelical Women and the Power of Submission* (Berkeley: University of California Press, 1997).

7 Rosemary Radford Ruether and Rosemary Skinner Keller, eds., *Women and Religion in America*, 3 vols. (San Francisco: Harper & Row, 1981–1986), 2:161.

8 Gerald F. Moran, " 'Sisters in Christ': Women and the Church in Seventeenth-Century New England," in *Women in American Religion*, ed. Janet Wilson James (Philadelphia: University of Pennsylvania Press, 1976), 47–65; Laurel Thatcher Ulrich, "Vertuous Women Found: New England Ministerial Literature, 1668–1735," in James, *Women in American Religion*, 67–88. Ruth H. Bloch, "The Gendered Meanings of Virtue in Revolutionary America," *Signs: Journal of Women in Culture and Society* 13, no. 1 (1987): 37–58. See Jan Lewis, "The Republican Wife: Virtue and Seduction in the Early Republic," *William and Mary Quarterly*, 3rd ser., 44, no. 4 (1987): 689–721. Susan Juster writes, "The restoration of agency is the key to understanding women's experience of grace. . . . These women were empowered by recovering their sense of self through the assertion of independence from others." Juster, " 'In a Different Voice': Male and Female Narratives of Religious Conversion in Post-Revolutionary America," *American Quarterly* 41, no. 1 (1989): 53.

9 Ruether and Keller, *Women and Religion in America*, 1:34.

10 Ruether and Keller, *Women and Religion in America*, 2:402, 1:36; Catharine E. Beecher and Harriet Beecher Stowe, *The American Woman's Home; or, Principles of Domestic Science; being a Guide to the Formation and Maintenance of Economical Healthful Beautiful and Christian Homes* (New York: J. B. Ford; Boston: H. A. Brown, 1869), 19.

11 For one particularly well known example, see Beecher and Stowe, *American Woman's Home*, 28–29. See also Sandra S. Sizer, *Gospel Hymns and Social Religion: The Rhetoric of Nineteenth-Century Revivalism* (Philadelphia: Temple University Press, 1978), chap. 4. Alexis de Tocqueville, *Democracy in America*, ed. Henry Steele Commager, trans. Henry Reeve (New York: Oxford University Press, 1947), 401, 403. Ann Douglas, *The Feminization of American Culture* (New York: Knopf, 1977).

12 Mary P. Ryan, "A Women's Awakening: Evangelical Religion and the Families of Utica, New York, 1800–1840," in James, *Women in American Religion*, 107.

13 Ruether and Keller, *Women and Religion in America*, 2:401.

14 Catharine E. Beecher, *A Treatise on Domestic Economy, for the Use of Young Ladies at Home, and at School* (Boston: T. H. Webb, 1841), 9. These ideas of Victorian domestic culture are developed nicely by Colleen McDannell, *The*

Christian Home in Victorian America, 1840–1900 (Bloomington: Indiana University Press, 1986).

15 McDannell, *Christian Home in Victorian America*, passim.

16 The "feminization" of American Protestantism in the nineteenth century extended well beyond the evangelical ambit, and so did the various reclamation efforts early in the twentieth; see Gail Bederman, " 'The Women Have Had Charge of the Church Work Long Enough': The Men and Religion Forward Movement of 1911–1912 and the Masculinization of Middle-Class Protestantism," *American Quarterly* 41, no. 3 (1989): 432–65; quoted in Douglas Frank, *Less than Conquerors: How Evangelicals Entered the Twentieth Century* (Grand Rapids: Eerdmans, 1986), 192; Ruether and Keller, *Women and Religion in America*, 3:260–62.

17 Marabel Morgan, *The Total Woman* (Old Tappan, N.J.: F. H. Revell, 1973), 55.

18 "Dr. Dobson Answers Your Questions," *Focus on the Family* 13 (1989): 8.

19 Quoted in Frances FitzGerald, *Cities on a Hill: A Journey through Contemporary American Cultures* (New York: Simon & Schuster, 1981), 29.

20 Quoted in Carol Flake, *Redemptorama: Culture, Politics, and the New Evangelicalism* (Garden City, N.Y.: Anchor, 1984), 70.

21 Quoted in Randall Balmer, *Mine Eyes Have Seen the Glory: A Journey into the Evangelical Subculture in America* (New York: Oxford University Press, 1989), 120–21.

22 Quoted in Flake, *Redemptorama*, 87; Beecher, *Treatise on Domestic Economy*, 13.

8: RE-CREATE THE NATION

1 Jerry Falwell, *Strength for the Journey: An Autobiography* (New York: Simon & Schuster, 1987), 334–35.

2 Quoted in Mark Tooley, *Methodism and Politics in the Twentieth Century* (Anderson, Ind.: Bristol House, 2012), 222, 224–25; *Annual of the Southern Baptist Convention, 1972* (Nashville: Southern Baptist Convention, 1972), 72. On the reaffirmations of the 1971 resolution, see *Annual of the Southern Baptist Convention, 1974* (Nashville: Southern Baptist Convention, 1974), 76. The 1976 resolution was more measured, calling on "Southern Baptists and all citizens of the nation to work to change those attitudes and conditions which encourage many people to turn to abortion as a means of birth control"; but it also affirmed "our conviction about the limited role of government in dealing with matters relating to abortion, and support the right of expectant mothers to the full range of medical services and personal counseling for the preservation of life and health." *Annual of the Southern Baptist Convention, 1976* (Nashville: Southern Baptist Convention, 1976), 58.

3   Quoted in "What Price Abortion?" *Christianity Today*, March 2, 1973, 39 [565].

4   "Abortion and the Court," *Christianity Today*, February 16, 1973, 32 [502]; quoted in "What Price Abortion?"; Floyd Robertson, *United Evangelical Action* (Summer 1973): 8–11 (quotes from 11).

5   For a superb review of the circumstances surrounding the *Green v. Kennedy* case, see Joseph Crespino, "Civil Rights and the Religious Right," in *Rightward Bound: Making America Conservative in the 1970s*, ed. Bruce J. Schulman and Julian E. Zelizer (Cambridge, Mass.: Harvard University Press, 2008), 90–105. Crespino correctly identifies this case, together with *Green v. Connally*, as the catalyst for the Religious Right.

6   *Green v. Connally*, 330 F. Supp. 1150 (D. D.C.) aff'd sub nom. *Coit v. Green*, 404 U.S. 997 (1971).

7   "The Moral Majority," undated paper, Box 19, Paul M. Weyrich Papers, American Heritage Center, University of Wyoming.

8   Quoted in William Martin, *With God on Our Side: The Rise of the Religious Right in America* (New York: Broadway, 1996), 173. As early as February 1979, several months before the formation of an organization by that name, Howard Phillips was using the term "moral majority"; see Phillips to Falwell, February 27, 1979, Evangelist Activism, Box 15, Paul M. Weyrich Papers, American Heritage Center, University of Wyoming. According to historian Robert Freedman, "The Supreme Court's banning of public school prayer (1962) and legalization of abortion (1973) outraged many evangelicals and fundamentalists. However, few decided to participate actively in politics as a result." He adds, "Weyrich believes that the Carter administration's policy toward Christian Schools was the turning point" (Freedman, "The Religious Right and the Carter Administration," *Historical Journal* 48, no. 1 [2005]: 236). Michael Lienesch writes, "The Christian conservative lobbyists were originally concerned with protecting the Christian schools from Internal Revenue Service investigations over the issue of racial imbalance" (Lienesch, "Right-Wing Religion: Christian Conservatism as a Political Movement," *Political Science Quarterly* 97, no. 3 [1982]: 409). On the importance of schools to the nascent Religious Right, see also J. Charles Park, "Preachers, Politics, and Public Education: A Review of Right-Wing Pressures against Public Schooling in America," *Phi Delta Kappan* 61, no. 5 (1980): 608–12.

9   "'Most Unusual': No Time for a Change," *Christianity Today*, December 17, 1971, 34. Bob Jones III insisted that "there was no connection between the enrollment of this one black student and the major threats facing the university."

10 Paul Weyrich, "The Pro-Family Movement," *Conservative Digest* 6 (1980): 14.

11 Freedman, "Religious Right and the Carter Administration," 238, 240; Wilfred F. Drake, "Tax Status of Private Segregated Schools: The New Revenue Procedure," *William and Mary Law Review* 20 (1979): 463–512; "Jimmy Carter's Betrayal of the Christian Voter," *Conservative Digest*, August 1979, 15; Michael Sean Winters, *God's Right Hand: How Jerry Falwell Made God a Republican and Baptized the American Right* (New York: HarperOne, 2012), 110; Crespino, "Civil Rights and the Religious Right," 99–100. For a look inside the evangelical subculture, see Randall Balmer, *Mine Eyes Have Seen the Glory: A Journey into the Evangelical Subculture in America*, 5th ed. (New York: Oxford University Press, 2014).

12 Freedman, "Religious Right and the Carter Administration," 240–41, 242; Duane Murray Oldfield, *The Right and the Righteous: The Christian Right Confronts the Republican Party* (Lanham, Md.: Rowman & Littlefield, 1996), 100.

13 Quoted in Michael Cromartie, ed., *No Longer Exiles: The Religious New Right in American Politics* (Washington, D.C.: Ethics and Public Policy Center, 1993), 26.

14 Quoted in Cromartie, *No Longer Exiles*, 26; quoted in Martin, *With God on Our Side*, 173. Falwell declared in his sermon, "The Roman Catholic church is to be commended for their diligent and persistent battle against abortion. They have done far more to my knowledge than any other one segment of our society, to try to stop abortion" (Falwell, sermon [transcript], "Abortion-on-Demand: Is It Murder," Gen 1:26, 27, February 26, 1978, SE-126, Liberty University Archives).

15 Quoted in Cromartie, *No Longer Exiles*, 52; Dan Gilgoff, "Exclusive: Grover Norquist Gives Religious Conservatives Tough Love," God & Country, *U.S. News & World Report*, June 11, 2009, accessed September 30, 2009, www.usnews.com/blogs/god-and-country/2009/06/11/exclusive-grover-norquist-gives-religious-conservatives-tough-love.

16 Elmer L. Rumminger, telephone interview with the author, July 17, 2010.

17 Douglas E. Kneeland, "Clark Defeat in Iowa Laid to Abortion Issue," *New York Times*, November 13, 1978; Dick Clark, interview with Bruce Morton, CBS News, November 13, 1978. See also Hedrick Smith, "A Pattern of Stability: With Incumbents Faring Well, Results Indicate that Fears of Voter Revolt Were Exaggerated," *New York Times*, November 8, 1978. Allegations later emerged that the white government of South Africa may have illegally contributed money toward Clark's defeat because of his strong stand against apartheid. Wendell Rawls Jr., "South African Role in Iowa Voting Charged," *New York Times*, March 22, 1979.

18 "Religion at the Polls: Strength and Conflict," *Christianity Today*, December 1, 1978, 40–41.

19 Georgia Glasman to Weyrich, January 26, 1978, Box 3, Paul M. Weyrich Papers, American Heritage Center, University of Wyoming.

20 Weyrich to Daniel B. Hales, December 31, 1978, Box 3, Paul M. Weyrich Papers, American Heritage Center, University of Wyoming; Robert "Bob" Billings, Christian School Action Inc., to Weyrich, December 6, 1978, Box 3, Paul M. Weyrich Papers, American Heritage Center, University of Wyoming.

21 Freedman, "Religious Right and the Carter Administration," 243; Billings to Weyrich.

22 Philip Yancey, "Schaeffer on Schaeffer, Part II," *Christianity Today*, April 6, 1979, 25.

23 Frank Schaeffer, *Crazy for God: How I Grew Up as One of the Elect, Helped Found the Religious Right, and Lived to Take All (Or Almost All) of It Back* (New York: Carroll & Graf, 2007), 283, 259, 293; Robert Maddox, interview with the author, Bethesda, Md., December 6, 2012. According to his son, Francis Schaeffer had initially balked at bringing up abortion because he didn't "want to be identified with some Catholic issue" (Schaeffer, *Crazy for God*, 266). The companion volume for the film series is Francis A. Schaeffer and C. Everett Koop, *Whatever Happened to the Human Race?: Exposing Our Rapid Yet Subtle Loss of Human Rights* (Old Tappan, N.J.: F. H. Revell, 1979). For a profile of Alonzo McDonald, see Mark Oppenheimer, "From One Benefactor, Diverse Seeds in Theology," *New York Times*, July 16, 2010. On the ubiquity of "secular humanism," see Tim LaHaye, *The Battle for the Mind* (Old Tappan, N.J.: F. H. Revell, 1980). LaHaye dedicated the book to Schaeffer. In his paean to Schaeffer, Cal Thomas declared, "No man contributed as much to the conservative side of the ideological battle than did Dr. Francis Schaeffer, who died of cancer last month at the age of 72" (Cal Thomas, transcript, Moral Majority Report, June 28, 1984, Liberty University Archives).

24 Quoted in Martin, *With God on Our Side*, 173.

9: HIS OWN RECEIVED HIM NOT

1 Memorandum, Paul Laxalt to Chuck Tyson, September 12, 1980, folder "Political Ops—Voter Groups—Christians/Evangelicals" (1/4), Box 255, Reagan, Ronald: 1980 Campaign Papers, 1965–80, Edwin Meese Files, Ronald Reagan Library. See also Nancy Gibbs and Michael Duffy, *The Preacher and the Presidents: Billy Graham in the White House* (New York: Center Street, 2007), chap. 25. The definitive study of Graham's political machinations is Steven P. Miller, *Billy Graham and the Rise of the Republican South* (Philadelphia: University of Pennsylvania Press, 2009).

2 Billy Graham to Bob Maddox, September 23, 1980, "Office of Public Liaison, Bob Maddox, Religious Liaison," Box 4, Jimmy Carter Library.

3 Regarding Graham's letter to John Kennedy and the Montreux meeting eight days later, see Randall Balmer, *God in the White House: How Faith Shaped the Presidency from John F. Kennedy to George W. Bush* (San Francisco: HarperOne, 2008), 28–29. Graham's own account of the *Life* article appears in Graham, *Just As I Am: The Autobiography of Billy Graham* (San Francisco: HarperSanFrancisco, 1997), 392–93. In his autobiography Graham says that he "wrote privately to both Kennedy and his running mate, Lyndon Baines Johnson, explaining why I was not going to vote for them"; he mentions nothing about his pledge not to raise the "religious issue" (392).

4 Gibbs and Duffy, *Preacher and the Presidents*, 262; Graham to President and Mrs. Carter, November 6, 1979, WHCF-Name File, Jimmy Carter Library. On the relatively distant relationship between Carter and Graham, see Gibbs and Duffy, *Preacher and the Presidents*, chap. 24.

5 Gibbs and Duffy, *Preacher and the Presidents*, 260–61; Memorandum, Maddox to President and Mrs. Carter, September 5, 1979, WHCF-Name File, Jimmy Carter Library; Adrian Rogers to Maddox, August 23, 1979, "Office of Public Liaison, Bob Maddox, Religious Liaison," Box 1, Jimmy Carter Library. The following year, Graham somewhat disingenuously told the *National Layman's Digest*, "I admire Jerry Falwell as a tremendous preacher of the gospel—but I didn't join the Moral Majority because I do not agree in taking the pulpit into politics and identifying certain people for defeat" (Graham, quoted in *National Layman's Digest*, October 15, 1981).

6 Gibbs and Duffy, *Preacher and the Presidents*, 261.

7 Robert Freedman, "The Religious Right and the Carter Administration," *Historical Journal* 48, no. 1 (2005): 249. According to some accounts, the leaders of the Religious Right also considered Philip M. Crane, U.S. representative from Illinois; Howard Baker, U.S. senator from Tennessee; and Jesse Helms, U.S. senator from North Carolina. See, for example, Memorandum, Anne Wexler and Maddox to Phil Wise, October 22, 1979, "Religious Matters," Box RM-1, WHCF-Subject File-General, Jimmy Carter Library. Falwell also confirmed that Connally was under consideration. See Cal Thomas and Ed Dobson, *Blinded by Might: Can the Religious Right Save America?* (Grand Rapids: Zondervan, 1999), 270. When Tim LaHaye caught wind that some conservatives were considering Connally, he objected vigorously. Writing to Weyrich about Connally, LaHaye said, "He is no born again Christian, is unelectable and has little or no conservative following in his home state" (note, LaHaye to Paul Weyrich, March 2, 1980, Paul M. Weyrich Papers, Box 4, American Heritage Center, University of Wyoming).

8 Jimmy Carter, *Our Endangered Values: America's Moral Crisis* (New York: Simon & Schuster, 2005), 40. Carter mistakenly attributed this remark to Rogers, not Smith; Carter apologized (Carter, interview with the author, Plains, Ga., June 2, 2013).

10: KEEP THE FAITH AND GO THE DISTANCE

1 Quoted in Douglas Frank, *Less than Conquerors: How Evangelicals Entered the Twentieth Century* (Grand Rapids: Eerdmans, 1986), 193; see Gail Bederman, "'The Women Have Had Charge of the Church Work Long Enough': The Men and Religion Forward Movement of 1911–1912 and the Masculinization of Middle-Class Protestantism," *American Quarterly* 41, no. 3 (1989): 432–65.

2 On the Power Team, see Sharon Mazer, "Power Team: Muscular Christianity and the Spectacle of Conversion," *The Drama Review* 38, no. 4 (1994): 162–88.

3 Ralph Reed, *Active Faith: How Christians Are Changing the Soul of American Politics* (New York: Free Press, 1996), 120. McCartney retired after the 1994 season "to spend time with his family and to pursue a closer personal relationship with God."

4 "Religious Extremism, Religious Truth," *Christian Century*, December 20–27, 1995, 1236.

5 For an example of this genre, see John R. Rice, *Bobbed Hair, Bossy Wives and Women Preachers: Significant Questions for Honest Christian Women Settled by the Word of God* (Wheaton, Ill.: Sword of the Lord, 1941). See also Margaret Lamberts Bendroth, *Fundamentalism and Gender: 1875 to the Present* (New Haven, Conn.: Yale University Press, 1993), esp. chap. 3.

6 On the tradition of evangelical activism, which derives primarily from the holiness-pentecostal wing of evangelicalism, see Donald W. Dayton, *Discovering an Evangelical Heritage* (Peabody, Mass.: Harper & Row, 1976), esp. chap. 8. See also Betty A. DeBerg, *Ungodly Women: Gender and the First Wave of American Fundamentalism* (Minneapolis: Fortress, 1990).

7 Thomas L. Friedman, "Buchanan for President," *New York Times*, December 24, 1995, 9.

8 Bendroth argues that much of the appeal of dispensational premillennialism (and its concomitant success in defining limited roles for women) derived from a quest for order among evangelicals late in the nineteenth century. See *Fundamentalism and Gender*, chap. 2.

9 Robert J. Samuelson, "Great Expectations," *Newsweek*, January 8, 1996, 27.

10 Quoted in Ron Fimrite, "Once Powerful, Still Proud," *Sports Illustrated*, October 14, 1996, 8.

11 I have borrowed many of these ideas from John M. Murrin's brilliant essay on this topic, "Rites of Domination: Princeton, the Big Three, and the Rise of Intercollegiate Athletics" (paper delivered at Princeton University, October 10, 1996).

12 The Promise Keepers' site has undergone revision since the page containing this quote was accessed.

13 Gary Smalley, "Five Secrets of a Happy Marriage," in *Seven Promises of a Promise Keeper*, ed. Al Janssen and Larry K. Weeden (Colorado Springs: Focus on the Family, 1994), 105.

14 Tony Evans, "Spiritual Purity," in Janssen and Weeden, *Seven Promises of a Promise Keeper*, 73, 79.

15 Edward Abbey, *Abbey's Road* (New York: Dutton, 1979), xvi. Emphasis in original.

16 For a textbook example of evangelical dualism, see James Davison Hunter, *Culture Wars: The Struggle to Define America* (New York: Basic, 1991).

11: DEAD STONES

1 The biblical references are John 17:21 and 1 Cor 3:4. For an appraisal of mainline Protestantism, see Randall Balmer, *Grant Us Courage: Travels along the Mainline of American Protestantism* (New York: Oxford University Press, 1996).

2 Quoted in John F. Wilson and Donald L. Drakeman, eds., *Church and State in American History: Key Documents, Decisions, and Commentary from the Past Three Centuries*, 3rd ed. (Boulder, Colo.: Westview, 2003), 21.

3 Quoted in Wilson and Drakeman, *Church and State*, 30, 31.

4 Quoted in Wilson and Drakeman, *Church and State*, 64.

5 Thomas Jefferson, *Political Writings*, ed. Joyce Appleby and Terence Ball (Cambridge: Cambridge University Press, 1999), 391.

6 Quoted in Wilson and Drakeman, *Church and State*, 69.

7 See Wilson and Drakeman, *Church and State*, 71.

8 Quoted in Wilson and Drakeman, *Church and State*, 87. Although the First Amendment called for disestablishment, several of the states retained their religious establishments into the early decades of the nineteenth century. Connecticut disestablished Congregationalism in 1818, and Massachusetts (the last state to do so) followed suit in 1833.

9 Some years ago, I was on a panel at Gordon College when one of the leaders of the Religious Right actually advocated a prescribed prayer from a different religion for every school day, a concession of sorts, I suppose, to religious pluralism.

10 Quoted in Wilson and Drakeman, *Church and State*, 74.

11 Rick Scarborough, *In Defense of Mixing Church and State* (Lufkin, Tex.: Vision America, 1999), 12.

12 Quoted in Wilson and Drakeman, *Church and State*, 21.

13 Quoted in Wilson and Drakeman, *Church and State*, 23, 22.

14 William G. McLoughlin, ed., *Isaac Backus on Church, State, and Calvinism: Pamphlets, 1754–1789* (Cambridge, Mass.: Belknap Press of Harvard University Press, 1968), 315, 324. Emphasis in original.

15 The text of Truett's address is widely available on the internet, including here: George W. Truett, "Baptists and Religious Liberty" (address, National Capitol, Washington, D.C., May 16, 1920), accessed December 3, 2015, http://www.mainstreambaptists.org/mob/truett_sermon.htm.

16 Curiously, however, when Moore filed his appeal with the Eleventh Circuit, he did not ask for a stay of Thompson's order to have the monument removed, a fairly routine request—and one routinely granted. Robert J. Varley, one of the lead attorneys for the plaintiffs, believes that Moore was spoiling all along for a legal confrontation (conversation with the author). After a failed bid for governor, Moore was elected chief justice a second time, in 2012.

17 Quoted in Wilson and Drakeman, *Church and State*, 75.

18 On Meese's role in popularizing this notion, see Lynette Clemetson, "Meese's Influence Looms in Today's Judicial Wars," *New York Times*, August 17, 2004, A1, A16.

19 Adam Cohen, "Is John Roberts Too Much of a Judicial Activist?" *New York Times*, August 27, 2005. For another example of "judicial activism" on the part of conservatives, how about *Bush v. Gore* in 2000?

20 Randall Balmer, "John Henry Goetschius and 'The Unknown God': Eighteenth-Century Pietism in the Middle Colonies," *Pennsylvania Magazine of History and Biography* 113, no. 4 (1989): 599.

21 U.S. Supreme Court, *Wallace v. Jaffree* (1985), no. 83–812.

22 Quoted in Wilson and Drakeman, *Church and State*, 22.

CREDITS

I should like to thank my friend Carey Newman and the superb staff at Baylor University Press for shepherding this book to publication. Several of these chapters have appeared elsewhere in earlier forms, and I'd like to acknowledge their provenance and express gratitude for permissions.

Chapters 1, 5, 6, and 7 previously appeared in Randall Balmer, *Blessed Assurance: A History of Evangelicalism in America* (Boston: Beacon Press, 1999). Rights were reassigned to the author on October 6, 2006.

Chapter 2 was originally published as Randall Balmer, "Willful Naïveté: American Evangelicalism and the Stone-Campbell Tradition," *Stone-Campbell Journal* 22 (2004): 211–23.

Chapter 3 appeared as Randall Balmer, "Casting Aside the Ballast of History and Tradition: White Protestants and the Bible in the Antebellum Period," in *African Americans and the Bible: Sacred Texts and Social Textures*, edited by Vincent L. Wimbush (New York: Continuum, 2000), 193–200. Used by permission of Bloomsbury Publishing.

Chapter 4 was previously published as Randall Balmer, "An End to Unjust Inequality in the World: The Radical Tradition of Progressive Evangelicalism," *Church History and Religious Culture* 94 (2014): 505–30.

Chapter 8: An earlier version appeared in Randall Balmer, "The Real Origins of the Religious Right," *Politico Magazine*, May 27, 2014, online: http://www.politico.com/magazine/story/2014/05/religious-right-real-origins-107133.

Chapter 10 originally appeared as Randall Balmer, "Keep the Faith and Go the Distance: Promise Keepers, Feminism, and the World of Sports," in *The Promise Keepers: Essays on Masculinity and Christianity*, ed. Dane S. Claussen (Jefferson, N.C.: McFarland, 2000), 194–203. Reprinted by permission of Dane S. Claussen.

ABOUT THE AUTHOR

Randall Balmer, an Episcopal priest, is the John Phillips Professor in Religion and director of the Society of Fellows at Dartmouth College. He is the author of more than a dozen books, including *Redeemer: The Life of Jimmy Carter* and *Mine Eyes Have Seen the Glory: A Journey into the Evangelical Subculture in America*, now in its fifth edition, which was made into an award-winning documentary for PBS.

INDEX